# LETTERS
## FROM CUBA
### *and Other Plays*

# LETTERS
# FROM CUBA
## *and Other Plays*

## Maria Irene Fornes

PAJ
PUBLICATIONS

New York

*Letters from Cuba and Other Plays* is published by PAJ Publications, P. O. Box 532, Village Station, New York, NY 10014.

PAJ Publications is distributed to the trade by Consortium Book Sales and Distribution, 800-283-3572.

Cover and book design by Susan Quasha
Cover painting (detail): Leandro Soto, *The Destiny of an Island*, acrylic on canvas, 2001.

LIBRARY OF CONGRESS CATALOGING-IN-PUBLICATION DATA

Fornes, Maria Irene.
  Letters from Cuba and other plays / Maria Irene Fornes.
    p. cm.
  ISBN-13: 978-1-55554-076-0
  1. Cuba—Drama. I. Title.
  PS3556.O7344L48 2007
  812'.54—dc22
                                    2007010970

FIRST EDITION, MAY 2007

# Contents

# Letters from Cuba

*Letters from Cuba* premiered at the Signature Theatre Company, 424 West 42nd Street, New York City, on February 20, 2000.

CAST

LUIS, Chris De Oni
FRAN, Tai Jimenez
MARC, Matthew Floyd Miller
JOSEPH, Peter Starrett
JERRY/GERARDO, Peter Van Wagner
ENRIQUE, Rick Wasserman

Signature Theatre Company, *Producer*
James Houghton, *Artistic Director*
Bruce E. Whitacre, *Managing Director*

Maria Irene Fornes, *Director*

Donald Eastman, *Set Designer*
Teresa Snider-Stein, *Costume Designer*
Matthew Fry, *Lighting Designer*
Kurt B. Kellenberger, *Sound Designer*

*The play takes place simultaneously in New York City and Cuba. The dominant part of the set is an apartment in New York. The apartment is enclosed by two walls stage right and left. The stage right wall has two windows, and the stage left wall has a panel that appears to be a part of the wall but can open. There is a small alcove upstage center. The stage right wall of the alcove has a "doggie door"—the bottom half of the wall can open. There are two doors on either side of the alcove on the upstage wall. The stage right door leads to a hallway and the stage left door leads to an offstage bedroom. Between the alcove and the stage left door is an airshaft flanked by two windows. There are two Japanese-style futons on the floor, one against each wall stage right and left. There is a drafting table downstage left against the wall, and two chairs that flank the alcove.*

*Above the apartment is "Cuba." Cuba is a rooftop represented by a two-foot high wall extending across the stage above the apartment. Actors enter and exit via a staircase upstage left, so that they can be seen as they reach the top of the stairs. There is a rope ladder stage right that extends down to the stage floor behind the New York apartment. It is also possible to cross over the wall and walk onto the ceiling over the alcove in the New York apartment.*

*In the apartment, there is a breakfast picnic for three set up on a mat center stage.*

# Scene 1

*As the lights come up,* JOSEPH *and* MARC *are onstage making final preparations for breakfast.*

MARC: I was thinking … how does one write a poem?

JOSEPH: Oh my God. How does one write a poem?

MARC: A good poem.

JOSEPH: You want to write a good poem?

MARC: Yes, wouldn't you?

JOSEPH: Yes.

*Pause.*

MARC: What is a good poem?

JOSEPH: I'll tell you what is a good poem.

"Sahara Dies"
Until the desert knows:
That water grows
His sands suffice.
But let him once suspect
that Caspian fact.
Sahara dies.
—Emily Dickinson

MARC: My God.

JOSEPH: I've been writing poetry. And I've been saying words in my head to see if word spirits would come, like move in, like to join other words that were there. If they would do that then, to see if they would come in to form a poem. I think that's how poems get written. I think that's how difficult things get done. We can't really do them. We can't do difficult things. We can do easy things. But the difficult ones come to us by themselves. It's just that to learn to listen to them is difficult. We just have to learn to listen and to let them come in easy as if the words would come out by themselves because they want to make a poem. Because they desire to make a poem. As if words had desires, and they want to join other words to express something ... of beauty or longing or despair.

You'd like to write a poem.

MARC: Yes.

JOSEPH: Have you?

MARC: Yes. I tried.

JOSEPH: And ... was it good?

MARC: Yes, it was good.

JOSEPH: Can I read your poetry?

MARC: You want to read my poetry?

JOSEPH: Yeah, I want to read it.

MARC: I don't know.

JOSEPH: You don't know what?

MARC: No.

JOSEPH: Did you write one poem, or did you write many poems?

MARC: If you write one, you can write many.

*MARC puts the rose in his teeth and dances as Cuban music begins to play. FRAN enters and the three sit down to breakfast as lights crossfade to Cuba.*

## Scene 2

*LUIS sits on the wall and reads a letter he has written.*

LUIS: Dear Francisquita,

In spite of my long silence, you've been in my mind. I have not written because nothing is very interesting in my life. I wrote you three weeks ago and then 15 days ago.

Each time I looked at the letter, I felt embarrassed.
I tried to be cheerful, but it sounded insincere.
Last week I visited Titi. She's very well.

In your last letter, you told me that you went to the Metropolitan Museum with a friend and imagined I was there looking at the paintings with you. What a lovely thought. I wish I had been there with you.

Your loving brother,
Luis

## Scene 3

*New York. MARC, JOSEPH, and FRAN clean up the breakfast picnic.*

MARC: I think we should value life.

JOSEPH: What did you say?

MARC: I was thinking there are two things. One first. Then the other. First there's nothing. Then there's life. Then, it stops. And that's it. That's death. It is nothing again.

JOSEPH: Too many people believe in the afterlife for it to be false.

MARC: Well, but has anyone seen it, been there? Have any of them been there?

JOSEPH: A lot of them have. They say they have.

MARC: I wrote a poem about life.

> Death is a fact.
> First you're alive, then you're dead.
> You can't deny that because you can't.
> You value life because it's it.
> Be tender to it.
> Don't be demanding.
> Don't be clumsy with it.
> Be appreciative.
> Do the best you can.
> Don't go around saying
> that things are like this
> and things are like that,
> complaining.
> Worship it as one would worship
> an angel that comes in through the window
> and is sitting there in your room.
> Or sits on your lap.
>
> Angels do sit on peoples' laps
> when they need to advise you,
> They sit quietly,
> so don't start getting up
> and doing something you think is important and is not.
>
> Life is tender as an infant.
> It's like a newborn baby.
> Even tender like a newborn bird. As frail as that.
> We expect things from it.
> But it's us who have to take care of it.
> We ask it to do things for us.
> But we should do things for it.

JOSEPH: Yes.

MARC: That's what I think.

JOSEPH: Yes.

MARC: That's what I think.

JOSEPH: You're right Marc. One should value life.

# Scene 4

LUIS *reads a letter in Cuba.* FRAN *seems to hear his voice and gazes at him through the stage left window. After a few lines of the letter she exits through the bedroom door.*

LUIS: Dear Francisquita,

Enrique Ferrara was born December 20th. Five and a half pounds and a little less than a month early. I must tell you he is the laziest baby in the world. He has been sleeping for ten days, paying no attention to anyone or anything around him. Ana and I may now try to leave the country with our newly born.

When I get to New York, we'll talk all night long till the sun comes out. I keep postponing making the decision to go.

FRAN *appears at the top of the stairs in Cuba and reaches out for* LUIS.

But I know there will be no end to the pleasure of being with you there and talking through the night. It is now three in the morning and Ana sleeps. She turns to me and says, "Did you finish the letter?"

Love,
Luis

LUIS *turns and reaches for* FRAN *as she backs down the stairs with her arm still outstretched.*

# Scene 5

*Lights up in New York.* JOSEPH *sits in the chair stage right and plays the guitar, picking up the melody of the Cuban music that has just faded away.* MARC *lies on his futon.* FRAN *enters through the bedroom door and sees* JOSEPH. *He begins to play different music as she dances, then speaks as she continues to move.*

FRAN: Martha Graham said Ruth St. Denis was a deeply religious being. And she was a performer. Once, while dancing an East Indian dance, she dropped a rose. At first Martha thought it was an accident, but it was planned.

Why did she decide to drop the rose … ?

Martha was puzzled.

She learned that those moments in a dance can make it magic.

# Scene 6

*LUIS fans himself in Cuba.*

LUIS: Dear sister,

It is 8 A.M., and already the heat is intense. We were told this summer would be unbearable. It is. Not even the afternoon siesta has protected us from the midday heat. At this hour, we usually feel a breeze, but nothing moves. I understand the word "siesta" is the object of mockery in the U.S.A. They attribute it to a laziness and lack of purpose. The siesta is the opposite. It is a way of resting when the sun is unbearable and returning to work when the heat relents. Our workday starts at 8 A.M. and again at 6 P.M.

Love,
Luis

# Scene 7

*As FRAN starts to enter the apartment through the hallway door, LUIS tosses a letter down to her. She catches it and enters the apartment, reading the letter as LUIS reads softly in the background, coming out onto the roof directly over the New York apartment.*

FRAN/LUIS: Dear Francisca,

Awhile ago, Ana said to me, "Write a long letter to your sister Fran." And here I am now writing to you some of the many thoughts, ideas, and words I have spoken to you in my mind.

Last week, we received a notice for a package that was sent to us from New York. Ana and I were walking to the post office to pick up the package when we saw a woman walking in front of us. She was wearing gray stockings. Ana saw them and said, "I wish I had some stockings. I have no stockings. I would love to have gray stockings like that woman has."

We reached the post office and picked up the package. In it, there were stockings for Ana. Those stockings were in the very color we had just seen on the woman walking in front of us. How odd—there they were in that package. It was an impossible thing, and yet, there they were in that box coming from New York, the stockings Ana wanted.

Ana said, "I wish Francisca were here to give her a hug." The rest of the things we distributed evenly. We kept most of the dried soups. They were good for Ana's delicate stomach.

I saw Uncle Oscar. He had difficulty walking. I was concerned. Uncle Virgilio seems to be doing well.

Ana and I are trying our best.

Saludos,
Luis

# Scene 8

*Lights crossfade back to Cuba. It is dusk.* LUIS *and* ENRIQUE *are on the roof. They look up at the stars and enjoy the early evening breeze. Music plays.*

ENRIQUE: Why is Mars red papa?

LUIS: You want to hear the fairy tale version or the real version?

ENRIQUE: I want to hear the fairy tale version and I also want to hear the real version. But I want to hear the fairy tale version first.

LUIS: The fairy tale version is that Mars blushed when he saw a very lovely fairy star.

ENRIQUE: Why did he do that?

LUIS: He fell in love.

ENRIQUE: He fell?

LUIS: No. When you fall in love, you don't fall, you fly and then you blush.

ENRIQUE: What is blush?

LUIS: You feel hot in your face.

ENRIQUE: Hot?

LUIS: Yes.

ENRIQUE: That hurts.

LUIS: It doesn't hurt.

ENRIQUE: Hot hurts.

LUIS: Not that kind of hot. That kind of hot feels good.

ENRIQUE: Are you sure?

LUIS: I'm sure. Love makes you feel good.

ENRIQUE: How do you do that?

LUIS: Feel good?

ENRIQUE: Blush.

LUIS: You don't do it. You blush when you're sensitive.

ENRIQUE (*Softly*): I'm sensitive ... I'm very, very sensitive ...

It's difficult.

LUIS: What is difficult?

ENRIQUE: I don't like difficult.

*LUIS ad libs "What is difficult?"*

(*Very loud.*) It's difficuuuuult!

*Plaintive.*

Why? oh, why? is life so difficult?

LUIS: It just is. It's difficult.

ENRIQUE: Let's not do difficult. Let's do happy!

LUIS: You like saying "let's not do difficult."

ENRIQUE: Yes, let's not do difficult. Now you say it.

Let's sing the Moon Song!

*They dance and sing the song.*

LUIS/ENRIQUE: How I love the moon's bellybutton.
Oh how sweet it was to sleep on her back.
How I loved the moon's bellybutton.
When she rocked by the light of the stars.
I loved to sleep on her eye.
I loved to rock at her side.
How I love the moon's bellybutton
When I go to sleep at her siiiiiiide.

# Scene 9

*New York. MARC and JOSEPH asleep on their futons. JOSEPH is having a nightmare and is tossing and turning, making sounds that wake MARC. MARC goes to see what is the matter.*

MARC: Joseph? Joe? Joseph?

*JOSEPH pushes MARC away as he wakes up.*

JOSEPH: Are you okay?

MARC: Yes.

JOSEPH: Good.

MARC: Where is Fran?

JOSEPH: She went out.

MARC: Where did she go?

JOSEPH: I don't know. I love Fran.

MARC: I love her, too.

JOSEPH: You do?

MARC: Of course.

*FRAN enters through the hallway door, undetected by MARC and JOSEPH.*

JOSEPH: I love her, though.

MARC: So do I.

JOSEPH: Not the way I love her.

MARC: Yes, I do.

JOSEPH: No, you don't understand.

MARC: Yes, I understand.

JOSEPH: No, Marc, I love her.

MARC: I love her.

JOSEPH: What do you mean?

MARC: I mean that I love her a lot.

JOSEPH: Not the way I love her.

MARC: I don't know how you love her, but I love her a lot.

*The argument escalates into a pillow fight center stage. FRAN slams the door so MARC and JOSEPH will know she's there. They freeze, still holding their pillows.*

FRAN: Hi boys.

MARC/JOSEPH: Hi.

*FRAN goes to her room. Pillow fight continues. FRAN comes out of the bedroom having dropped off a few things and put on a jacket. The pillow fight stops.*

FRAN: Bye.

MARC/JOSEPH: Bye.

*She leaves.*

MARC: She's beautiful.

JOSEPH: I think she's seeing someone.

MARC: Dating?

JOSEPH: Well, yeah.

MARC: You think?

JOSEPH: Don't you think?

MARC: Yeah? Oh no. She rehearses at night.

JOSEPH: That late?

MARC: What do you mean?

JOSEPH: She comes home late.

MARC: She works late.

JOSEPH: Hm. She used to come like straight home from work ... or from class if she had a class.

MARC: That's true.

JOSEPH: Yeah. (*Pause.*) She used to stay home more. She used to be more ... like closer to us ... you know? We used to spend more evenings here ... we cooked, and ate dinner together ... and we went out together—How long has it been since we went out together?

MARC: Yeah. It seems that we haven't been out together for some time. It's schedule, I think. We have different schedules.

JOSEPH: Yeah. That's true. Schedule can ruin things. Like sometimes I work in the morning and you work in the afternoon and she works Sundays, or yeah, that's what it is. It's silly, but well, it's true ... schedule can ruin relationships.

MARC: Well, I don't think it's ruined. I don't think our relationship is ruined. We still do things together.

JOSEPH: Like what?

MARC: Like what? We're together all the time.

JOSEPH: It doesn't seem to me that we're together all the time.

MARC: We see each other all the time.

JOSEPH: I don't think we see each other all the time.

MARC: Of course we don't see each other all the time. Are you talking about seeing each other all the time? Day and night? Every hour of the day?!

JOSEPH: Yes, I am talking about seeing each other every hour of the day!

MARC: I don't know if I want us to see each other every hour of the day.

*Short pause.*

JOSEPH: Well, I do.

MARC: What for?!

JOSEPH: Never mind, Marc. You don't understand.

MARC: What do you mean we don't understand each other? We understand each other.

You know something, friendship is more lasting that romantic love.

JOSEPH: I agree.

MARC: How come?

JOSEPH: It lasts longer. Romantic love starts faster. It burns faster. And it ends faster.

MARC: Romantic love can grow roots.

JOSEPH: Yes. They're tender though. Romantic love can be lasting. But the love of a friend is the most lasting. It is.

MARC: Isn't that something.

# Scene 10

*New York. There is a loud knock on the hallway door. The door opens and JERRY enters. He is carrying two parking violations, a Polaroid picture, and a letter.*

JERRY: (*He waves a parking violation.*) Look at this. Take a look at this. Look at it.

JOSEPH: What is it?

JERRY: Look at it.

JOSEPH: What is it?

JERRY: Look at it, Joe. This is my answer.

"I am enclosing two Notices of Violation which I received unjustly on October 25th."

"This parking violation was left attached to the windshield wiper of my car. As you see in the photo,"

JOSEPH *looks at the photo.* JERRY *continues reading.*

"my car was two feet from the yellow line as witnessed by H.E.W. Jones—"

JOSEPH: Who is H.E.W. Jones?

JERRY: A neighbor, H.E.W. Jones, a friend who lives down the block. His name is H.E.W. Jones. And he witnessed the whole thing.

*Reading.*

" … who was present when I took the photos 15 minutes after receiving the second notice …

"Besides the falsehood of the statement of fault one can see the blatant disparity of the number of feet I was from the hydrant. In the first summons, written at 4:15 A.M., it is noted that the distance between the end of the yellow line and the back of my car is eight feet. And on the second summons written at 6:38 A.M. the distance is seven feet. Are you suggesting that I woke up sometime between 4:15 and 6:38 and moved the car one foot closer to the hydrant? Did the hydrant move closer to my car? Given the evidence it is my hope that you will cancel this summons. Yours truly, Jerry Corner. My address telephone number, driver's license number, etc."

How's that?

JOSEPH: That's good. I'm sure they'll honor that.

JERRY: Thank you.

# Scene 11

*LUIS reads a letter in Cuba while FRAN dances below in New York.*

LUIS: Dear Francisca,

Let me tell you what I've been thinking. It's about love. I see it as a concrete thing. I think of it with a shape, weight, color, and movement. It's a sphere. The color is pearl gray. It floats, even if its weight is heavier than air. It takes shape at a distance from the beloved. When it reaches the beloved, it touches him lightly. Then, it retreats and remains at a certain distance, modestly and silently.

Last time you wrote was in August. You owed me a letter since March. I thought it was an eternity. Now I am answering you in July. I hope our writing records will improve.

Amor,
Luis

# Scene 12

*FRAN goes to JOSEPH, who is sitting in the stage left chair.*

FRAN: Well some people understand words better than anything else. Other people understand color, other people understand sounds, I understand movement when I see things that I think other people understand. Music and movement.

The greatest gift a person can have is to be satisfied with the life they have. I want to feel satisfaction with the life I have. We should enjoy the life we have.

*FRAN tweaks JOSEPH on the cheeks. He jumps up and she runs out through the bedroom door and he chases her out. She runs back in and runs around and out the stage right airshaft window. JOSEPH quickly follows and gazes out the stage left window.*

# Scene 13

*LUIS reads a letter in Cuba.*

LUIS: Dear Francisquita,

I hear it is possible to travel to the States through Mexico. I will attempt to do that. First of all, I need to get a Mexican visa. To get a Mexican visa, I must present a legalized birth certificate. To get this, I must have the date, volume, and folio of my registration and the number and address of the registry where it was filed. I must have all this on hand when I'm called to appear ... without this, I will not be able to travel. I hope the registration information is in one of the folders Mother keeps in her files.

Love,
Luis

# Scene 14

*Cuba. It is dusk. LUIS sits on the roof singing to himself.*

ENRIQUE: (*Offstage, calling.*) Papa!

LUIS: (*Still inspired, he finishes the phrase.*) Here ... !

ENRIQUE: Where are you?

LUIS: Here!

ENRIQUE: Gerardo's here.

LUIS: What does he want?

ENRIQUE: Gerardo, what do you want?

GERARDO: What do you mean, "what do I want?" I'm just coming to say hello. Why does he ask what I want? Can't someone just come and say hello? What's the matter with him?

ENRIQUE: Papa, what's the matter with you?

LUIS: What's the matter with me?

ENRIQUE: Papa, Gerardo wants to know what's the matter with you.

LUIS: There's nothing the matter with me. What's the matter with him?!

ENRIQUE: There's nothing the matter with him. We're going to play baseball.

LUIS: Gerardo?! You're going to play baseball with Gerardo?!

ENRIQUE: Yeah. Gerardo's the pitcher.

LUIS: Gerardo?! The pitcher. You don't need him to play baseball. You can play baseball with me. What's the matter with you? You don't think your Papa can play baseball?! Come here.

ENRIQUE: What for?

LUIS: I'm going to teach you h-h-h-how to play baseball. Didn't you want to learn to play baseball? Come up.

ENRIQUE: What for?

LUIS: You come up, or I'll come down.

ENRIQUE: I don't want to come down.

LUIS: You come up then.

ENRIQUE: I don't want to.

LUIS: I'm coming down.

ENRIQUE: Oh my God, Papa, look down there.

LUIS: Look at what?

ENRIQUE: Down there Papa!

ENRIQUE *appears on the roof as* LUIS *goes down the stairs.*

LUIS: Come back here.

ENRIQUE: You come here.

LUIS: Spoiled brat.

ENRIQUE: Papa. Don't talk so loud, people will hear you.

LUIS: Come here.

ENRIQUE: Gerardito's here.

LUIS: Good afternoon, Gerardo. Come up.

*There is a loud crashing sound.*

GERARDO (*Off*):
  Avemaríapurisma!
  Ouch—ouch—ouch.
  I'm okay. I'm okay.

ENRIQUE (*Off*):
  Oops! He tripped.
  Are you okay, Herry?
  Papa! Gerardito fell down!

LUIS: Enrique, get the Ben Gay.

ENRIQUE: Yeah, Papa. I'll get the Ben Gay.

*ENRIQUE runs back down the stairs again.*

ENRIQUE: Ben Gay! Papa, where is the Ben Gay?

LUIS: It's in the cabinet.

ENRIQUE: What cabinet?

LUIS: In the kitchen.

ENRIQUE: Okay.

*To GERARDO.*

  Are you okay, Herry?

*ENRIQUE helps GERARDO onto the roof. GERARDO wears a military uniform.*

*GERARDO grunts.*

LUIS: You want to sit down?

*GERARDO grunts.*

LUIS: You want to sit down or not!?

*GERARDO mumbling.*

LUIS: Herry, what do you want?

*GERARDO mumbling.*

ENRIQUE: I got the Ben Gay.

LUIS: What happened, Herry?

*GERARDO mumbles.*

LUIS: Can you come up?

*GERARDO mumbles.*

LUIS: You want me to help you?

*GERARDO mumbles.*

LUIS: Help him, Enrique.

*There are some sounds of pain as they are coming up. LUIS and GERARDO appear on the roof. GERARDO wears a Miliciano uniform.*

GERARDO: Patria o muerte!

ENRIQUE: What does that mean?

LUIS: You don't want to know. Okay, sit down. How's your back?

GERARDO: It's better. (*He sits.*) Yeah. It's better.

LUIS: How's your pitching arm?

GERARDO: Not so good.

*ENRIQUE rubs Ben Gay into GERARDO's back.*

## Scene 15

*MARC sits in the stage right chair writing. JOSEPH is at the drafting table.*

MARC: What's the matter?

*JOSEPH looks at MARC. There is a moment's pause.*

I thought something was wrong.

*JOSEPH shakes his head.*

JOSEPH: Why?

MARC: Because you looked odd.

*MARC goes back to work. JOSEPH looks at the floor. They are silent awhile.*

JOSEPH: I looked odd?

MARC: Yeah.

JOSEPH: How odd?

MARC: Well, odd.

JOSEPH: Odd? Like this?

*He makes an odd face.*

MARC: No.

JOSEPH: (*Making different odd faces.*) Like this? Like this?

*JOSEPH continues making faces. Each time JOSEPH makes a face, MARC says "No."*

JOSEPH: Like this?

MARC: Stop it.

JOSEPH: Like this?

MARC: Joseph, stop it.

*JOSEPH makes one last face. This one has the air of one who is rejected. MARC looks at JOSEPH.*

JOSEPH: Where is Fran?

MARC: … I don't know …

JOSEPH: She's not in? Where is she?

MARC: I don't know.

*JOSEPH rests his head on MARC's knee.*

JOSEPH: I'm cold.

MARC: What, Joseph?

JOSEPH: Have you noticed anything?

MARC: About what?

JOSEPH: Fran.

MARC: Does she know?

JOSEPH: I haven't told her.

MARC: You haven't told her?

JOSEPH: No.

MARC: Are you going to?

JOSEPH: I don't think so.

MARC: Can I tell her?

JOSEPH: Not just yet.

MARC: Why?

JOSEPH: Because it may spoil something.

MARC: What?

JOSEPH: Maybe friendship.

MARC: Hmm. The three of us.

JOSEPH: Oh no ... you think ... ? Oh I don't ... .

*Pause.*

> Except I don't know if she feels the same way. I know she cares for me as a friend. But does she love me the way I love her? Did you notice anything about that? Do you think she notices that I feel this way? That sometimes when I'm talking to you, I am looking at her?

MARC: No, I didn't notice.

JOSEPH: And sometimes when I look at her, I just stare. I always looked at her. Just thought I liked her. Until one day, it hit me. Like "bang." I love her. Oh, how I love her. Have you seen her dance? I know she loves me. But will she ever say it? Would she ever say, "I love you? I love you, Joe"? She loves me as a friend. But will she ever say, "I love you, Joe"?

# Scene 16

*Cuba. LUIS and GERARDO enter together and sit on the wall in silence. GERARDO holds a cup of atole in his hand. He eats the atole with a spoon. He is downcast.*

GERARDO: Patria o Muerte.

*LUIS mumbles.*

GERARDO: Luis, everyone I knew is gone. Everyone but you.

LUIS: Hmm. Yes, Gerardo ... Most of the ones close to me are gone too ...

GERARDO: You may be leaving too.

LUIS: I don't know, Gerardo. For some it's harder to leave. Francisquita left. All my brothers and sisters left. Cousins, uncles, nephews. Some are ... fearful, or ... just not capable or starting ... starting anew ... maybe fearful of that separation ... what we know ... have always known ... where we have always been ... not capable of taking a step ... separating ourselves from what we know ... from what is familiar ... and close to our hearts ... not capable of starting ... starting to coexist with an unfamiliar world ... something inside fearful ... something that makes one ... like cripples ... sort of. The young are eager ... But for us, the eagerness goes. We prefer what is familiar ... and remember the past.

GERARDO: My parents worked hard. They saved and opened a feed store. They sold tools and seeds. I want to leave. I prepared my application to leave. I've done this many times. But I've never put it in. When you apply to leave, you lose your job. And your rations. And while you wait for a permit to travel, your family has to take care of you. And this is hard on them. But there is another reason why I haven't put it in. I came here when I was young. But I still feel if I left here, I would die. Because I belong here, and if I went elsewhere, I wouldn't recognize anything around me and I would die. So many leave and seem to be happy elsewhere. They write letters saying they are happy. In Miami, in Spain, in Mexico. But I don't know that I could be happy in any of those places. So, I stay. As hard as things are here, I must stay. I know every building in this neighborhood, and every pothole in the streets. Half the people in the neighborhood were born when I was a young man. I saw them grow. I knew their parents, grandparents and their problems. And I went to their birthday parties. And if I leave, I would be among strangers all the time. And even if they are nice to me, I would not know who they are.

## Scene 17

*American big band music plays.*

*LUIS climbs down the rope ladder and enters the New York apartment through the hallway door. FRAN enters through the bedroom door and stands stage left. LUIS wanders slowly through the apartment looking at everything. He gently touches FRAN's picture on the wall. He exits through the hallway door then quickly reenters through the hallway door again.*

*He dances with FRAN.*

## Scene 18

*New York. As American music plays, ENRIQUE enters New York through the doggie door and begins a little dance that ends with a big finish. He then notices the picture of FRAN on the wall and goes over to her.*

ENRIQUE: My little Tía Francisquita—

*Suddenly, the hallway door opens and ENRIQUE attempts to hide himself with the stage left futon. FRAN enters and retrieves her jacket from the hook upstage center. She starts to leave and ENRIQUE uncovers himself, thinking she is gone. She seems to remember something else and crosses to the drafting table. ENRIQUE quickly hides again. She retrieves a piece of paper from the table and continues gazing at it as she walks out the door. ENRIQUE gets up, now certain that she is really gone. He sits on the stage left windowsill and begins to talk to the picture.*

ENRIQUE: Francisquita—

Do you remember when you came and brought us different kinds of food? Dry food, that was good once we soaked it in water, and food in cans. You apologized and said that food in cans was not as good as fresh food, but that you were not allowed to bring fresh food through customs. But it turned out that we loved food in cans. Mmmm.

At first you thought we were being polite to you because that was what you brought. But we really meant it. We liked food in cans. It had an American taste. A little taste of tin. When we ate it, we thought we were in the U.S. and spoke English to each other. We said, "Thank you." "Water, please." "How do you do?" "Good morning." "What is your name?" "Do you speak Spanish?"

But also, it was good because we could use the cans as glasses to drink water, or pots to heat water for coffee or containers to put food in and save it in the refrigerator. We could make holes in the bottom and turn them into pots for plants. We grew beans, not too many, because the pots were small. And we also grew coffee. We kept one (without the holes) to put on the roof to collect water when it rains. Mother likes to wash her hair with rainwater. I kept another in my room to hit with a spoon as a cowbell to use when I play music with my group. We also keep a candle in the sardine can. When the lights go out, Mama lights the candle. We thank you for the light.

When you came, we thought you may not like how we lost electric power so many times in one evening, and we told you we were sorry. You cheered us up and said, "Oh, no! Look how beautiful the light of the candle is when the room is dark." We looked, and we saw that you were right. We all looked elegant. You said, "This is how fancy restaurants are lit in New York and Paris also." That did cheer us up and made us understand the irony of it. At home, we get depressed when we have to eat in the dark, and in rich places where they have electricity, they turn the lights off and light candles to make it look more elegant. So you see how much we have learned from you.

*ENRIQUE goes over to FRAN's picture and gives "her" a kiss. He then goes to pick up his ukulele and poses with it leaning against the wall.*

ENRIQUE: I'm going to sing you a little song.

*ENRIQUE sings "I Love a Piano" and accompanies himself on the ukulele.*

*JERRY enters simultaneously through the hallway door with MARC through the bedroom door to join ENRIQUE for the end of the dance. LUIS appears in Cuba dancing on his own with them. At the end of the dance, ENRIQUE turns upstage to LUIS.*

ENRIQUE: Papa, I want to be in New York!

*ENRIQUE exits through the window. MARC exits through the bedroom door and JERRY starts to follow him until FRAN enters through the hallway door.*

# Scene 19

JERRY: Good morning, Miss Fran.

FRAN: Good morning, Jerry.

JERRY: Am I too early for the class? Should I come later, or could I have my class now? Because I was on the block fixing a boiler … and I thought, if I could come over now. Are you sure it's okay?

FRAN: It's all right.

*They take positions opposite each other.*

FRAN: Arms up …

*They perform a brief pas de deux with FRAN coaching JERRY as they dance. After a final wave to each other, JERRY exits the apartment through the hallway door.*

# Scene 20

*Cuba/New York.*

LUIS: Today is my birthday.

FRAN: Happy birthday!

*FRAN exits through bedroom door.*

LUIS: Thank you.

I am fine except for a little cold and now I've given it to Enrique. Other than that, everyone is fine. Enrique, too skinny—and there is a hurricane a few miles away and it's headed this way. I am listening to the radio to see if we'll have to take shelter.

In any case, I wrote to you a few weeks ago. We don't know if you got the letter. Nor do we know if this one will reach you.

We did receive your package with some clothes and a bottle with aspirins and some red pills. Some of the aspirins were crushed, but we can still use them. We don't know what the red pills are. I assume they are vitamins.

We will wait for your answer before taking them even if the mail takes
forever to arrive.

Love,
Luis

## Scene 21

JOSEPH *and* FRAN *enter,* FRAN *through the hallway door and* JOSEPH *through the
bedroom door.* JOSEPH *speaks as* FRAN *dances.*

JOSEPH: It's very hard to dance the woman in red.
    She has a curious form, a strange vulnerability.
    She's breathless.
    She's misunderstood.
    It's her eroticism they don't understand.
    She rocks from side to side
    on and on.
    A freeze in motion
    A constant rediscovery.
    Of a single moment.

FRAN *and* JOSEPH *move toward each other as the lights crossfade to Cuba.*

## Scene 22

*Cuba/New York.* LUIS *is on the roof.* ENRIQUE'S *voice is heard from offstage.*

ENRIQUE: Papi!

    Papi, come.

    I want you to come.

    Papi, I want you to come.

    Papi please.

    I can't go without you Papi.

    Papi, come.

    Come, papi.

*ENRIQUE leads LUIS into New York through the magic wall panel stage left.*

*LUIS crosses to FRAN. They embrace.*

*Lights fade.*

# *Terra Incognita*

## A libretto for an opera

FOR ROBERTO SIERRA

*Terra Incognita* originally premiered at The Women's Project &
Productions/INTAR, 420 West 42nd Street, New York City, on March 19,
1997.

CAST

AMALIA, Jennifer Alagna
CRISTOBAL, Lawrence Craig
BARTOLOME, John Muriello
ROB, Matthew Perri
GEORGIA, Candace Rogers-O'Connor

Women's Project & Productions, *Producer*
Julia Miles, *Artistic Director*

Roberto Sierra, *Music*

Maria Irene Fornes, *Director*
Stephen Gosling, *Musical Director*

Van Santvoord, *Set Designer*
Philip Widmer, *Lighting Designer*
Willa Kim, *Costume Designer*

The libretto was developed for presentation as a play at the Dionysia World
Theatre Festival, Siena, Italy, May, 1992.

CAST

Shawna Casey
Kimberly Flynn
Leo Garcia
Leon Martell
Steve Hofvendahl

Maria Irene Fornes, *Director*

The piece was also developed at the Padua Hills Playwrights Festival, July
1994.

CAST

Jennifer Alagna
Kimberly Flynn
Leo Garcia
Leon Martell
Steve Hofvendahl

Maria Irene Fornes, *Director*

## CHARACTERS

AMALIA: A delicate and intelligent American of Spanish descent. 28 years old.

GEORGIA: A curious and thoughtful American. 28 years old.

ROB: Amalia's brother. Sensitive and intelligent. Going through a difficult time emotionally. 29 years old.

BURT: A derelict. Cheerfully demented. Sometimes he recollects Christopher Columbus experiences.

STEVE: A man who sits in thoughtful repose. Except for the sailing speech he speaks words from Fray Bartolome de las Casas's *History of the Indies*, 1512.

*An outdoor café in the port of Palos, Spain. The building of the café is behind the audience. Upstage of the terrace is an elevation, a plateau, 10 to 15 feet high which extends beyond the width of the stage on both sides. Along the edge of the plateau is a dirt road. On the down side of the road and on the slope there are some trees, plants, and bushes. On the left there is a partial view of a kiosk. Next to the kiosk there is a milk crate. On the terrace, or lower level, there is a table and three chairs. On the table are two road maps, a travel brochure and magazine, a dictionary, a phrase book, a notebook, a pencil, a pen. Three American travelers in their mid-twenties are around the table. GEORGIA sits center, AMALIA sits left, ROB stands to GEORGIA's right looking over her shoulder at a travel brochure. After a few moments ROB sits on the milk crate.*

# Prince Henry

AMALIA: (*Reading what she just wrote.*) "Rob is getting coffee for himself and for me. Is Georgia getting coffee?"

*She turns to GEORGIA.*

Georgia ...

GEORGIA: Yes?

AMALIA: Are you getting coffee?

GEORGIA: Tea.

AMALIA: (*Writing.*) "Georgia is getting tea. Rob and I have not had an argument yet."

*GEORGIA laughs. AMALIA laughs.*

Have you?

*GEORGIA shakes her head. AMALIA writes.*

The day started well.
It's 9:20
and there's been no argument yet.

*AMALIA and GEORGIA look up toward ROB. ROB looks at them questioningly. He puts his hand to his ear. They put their thumbs to their own ears and wave their fingers. He points to them. Then, with finger pointed, he indicates circles around his ear and points to them again. He then waves and exits left. They wave back. AMALIA closes the diary. She is elated.*

I think we should drive
to Sagres tonight.
Let's go to the place
on the cliffs
where Prince
Henry built
his ships.

Let's go to the cliffs
where he thought
of ships
to sail
the ocean sea.

He did.

Is Prince Henry's castle still perched on those cliffs?

Let's go to Portugal,
Georgia.
Let's go tonight.

Does Prince Henry still sleep in a hair-shirt?

GEORGIA: Did he?

AMALIA: Yes.

*Pause.*

Do you know he died a virgin?

GEORGIA: No.

AMALIA: So they say.

*Pause.*

> He gathered men of knowledge—
> navigators from the East,
> from Greece, Syria, Egypt
> round him. Engineers,
> ship builders, instrument-makers.
> Inventors came to him,
> worked for him,
> from Greece, from Syria,
> from Egypt.
> Oh, Prince!
> The Navigator!

*She does a flamenco singer's intonation.* ROB *in mockery makes the sounds of a dog.*

> Let's leave him behind. Let's take the car and leave him behind. Oh, let's!

AMALIA *giggles.* GEORGIA *giggles.*

BOTH: Yes!

# A picture

GEORGIA *points to a picture in the brochure.*

GEORGIA: Look at this.

*She looks at the building behind the audience. Then, she looks at the pictures, and points to it again.*

> See this café?

*Pointing to it again.*

This café

*Pointing to the café downstage.*

is this café.

*Pointing to the picture.*

This here café

*Pointing to the café.*

is this café.

*Pointing to the picture.*

This here is our table.
You're sitting here.
I'm sitting here.
At this table.

*She points to another picture.*

See this?
It's a picture
of the inside
of the café.

*Pointing to the café.*

Of this café.

*Pointing to the picture.*

See the picture on the wall?—
It's a picture of the inside
of the café.

*Pointing to the café.*

Of this café.

On the wall of the café
in the picture, is a picture
of the inside of the café.

And in the picture of the inside of the café. On the wall of the café—

    is a picture of the inside of the café
     And on the wall of the café,
      in the picture
       of the inside
       of the café,
        is another picture
         of the inside of the café.
          And on the wall
           of that picture,
            of the picture
             of the inside
              of the café
               is again another picture
               of the inside
                of the café
                with
                 another picture
                  of the inside of the café.
Inside that picture
 of the inside of the café
  is again
    another picture
     of the picture of the picture
      of the picture
       of the picture
        of the picture
         of the picture

It's a picture of the picture
 of the inside of the café.

 A picture of the inside of the café;
  of the picture in the
   picture on the wall of the café.

Now, look here,
 the picture's just a dot
  on the wall of the café.

Now the picture
 is not even a dot.
  There is nothing on the wall
   of the café.

    Now there's just a dot.
     Then the dot is the café.

Now the dot is gone.

Puff.

No picture.
No wall.
And no café.

*Georgia and Amalia put their hands to their mouths and gasp in amazement.*

… Ahh …
      ahh
          ahh
              ahh

*They faint. Rob is on the top level. He holds a tray with drinks and a pile of old newspapers under his arm.*

Rob: Coffee!

*Amalia and Georgia walk a few steps up the slope. They take the cups from the tray and walk to the table. Amalia and Georgia sit.*

## A virgin

Rob: Why do you think Prince Henry died a virgin?

Amalia: Because he was dedicated.

*Rob sits.*

Rob: To what?

Amalia: To his work.

Rob: And what does virginity have to do with work?

AMALIA: … It helps.

ROB: It does not.

AMALIA: It does.

ROB: It does not.

AMALIA: Does.

ROB: Does not.

AMALIA: Does.

ROB: Does not.

AMALIA: Does.

| ROB: | AMALIA: |
|---|---|
| Not. Not. Not. Not. Not. | Does. Does. Does. Does. Does. |
| Not. Not. Not. Not. Not. | Does. Does. Does. Does. Does. |
| Not. Not. Not. Not. Not. | Does. Does. Does. Does. Does. |
| Not. Not. Not. Not. Not. | Does. Does. Does. Does. Does. |

*AMALIA opens her book. She mouths the words "first argument" as she writes. She looks at her watch. She mouths the words 9:23 as she writes.*

ROB: (*To himself.*) Not.

AMALIA: (*To herself.*) Does.

GEORGIA: Heavens!

*She looks at the brochure. ROB places a newspaper on the floor to the right of the table. He looks at the front page of the paper and places a stone on it. Through the following he repeats this until he has placed seven papers on the floor.*

## Isabel

GEORGIA: (*Looking at a brochure.*) Why do Spaniards say Isabel?

AMALIA: Why not?

GEORGIA: For Elizabeth. Why don't they say Isabella?

AMALIA: Because Isabella is not Spanish for Elizabeth.

GEORGIA: I thought that's how you say Elizabeth in Spanish.

AMALIA: No.

GEORGIA: Queen Isabella.

AMALIA: No.

GEORGIA: That's what I thought.

AMALIA: Well, it isn't.

GEORGIA: Oh.

AMALIA: You think the "La"
            in "La" Católica
            is part of Isabel.

            It's the "La"
            of "La" Católica.
            that makes you
            think that.

            It's Isabel "La"
            Católica.
            Not Isabela.
            That's all.

GEORGIA: ... Not Isabella?

AMALIA: No!  It's Isabel!

   Not.
   La, lalala-lalala lala
   La, lalala-lalala lala
   La, lalala-lalala lala

   But
   La, lalala-lalala lala
   La, lalala-lalala lala
   La, lalala-lalala lala

   It's
   La, lalala-lalala lala

La, lalala-lalala lala
La, lalala-lalala lala

Ca tó li ca.

BOTH: Not
La, lalala-lalala lala
La, lalala-lalala lala
La, lalala-lalala lala

But
La, lalala-lalala lala
La, lalala-lalala lala
La, lalala-lalala lala

It's
La, lalala-lalala lala
La, lalala-lalala lala
La, lalala-lalala lala

Ca tó li ca.

AMALIA: That's what it is.

GEORGIA: I see.

AMALIA: They even call the Infanta of Castile an elephant.

GEORGIA: An elephant?! Who does?

AMALIA: The English do. They call the poor Infanta an elephant.

GEORGIA: Is she fat?

AMALIA: She's not fat.

GEORGIA: Who is the Infanta of Castile?

AMALIA: The Princess Heiress of Spain.

GEORGIA: Do you mean Elephant and Castle?

AMALIA: Yes.

GEORGIA: Is that what Elephant and Castle means?

AMALIA: Yes.

GEORGIA: Oh, dear.

AMALIA: That's right.

# Amerigo

AMALIA: Like Amerigo
  which is
    what
    America comes from
    and sounds American
    but it's not

GEORGIA: Not American?

AMALIA: It's Italian.

GEORGIA: Italian?

AMALIA: Amerigo Vespucci.

GEORGIA: United States of Amerigo Vespucci?

AMALIA: Sí.

GEORGIA: The word America is not a Greek word or something?

AMALIA: Greek ... ?

GEORGIA: Something that means ... Nirvana or ... New World ... or land of possibility?

AMALIA: No.

*Reading in the magazine.*

> Vespucci, Amerigo, 1454-1512, Italian Navigator. Discovered and explored the mouths of the Amazon River in 1499 and sailed along the north shore of South America.

GEORGIA: Not North America?

AMALIA: ... No.

*She reads.*

The name America was used to honor him.

GEORGIA: Used to name South America?

AMALIA: North America, too.

GEORGIA: I see.

*AMALIA looks at the travel magazine.*

AMALIA: Listen to this. This is a puzzle.

*Reading.*

Two women have just met.
Woman 1: Were you ever in The States before?
Woman 2: No never.
Woman 1: Did you just come from Spain?
Woman 2: No, I've been traveling in America for the last two years.
Woman 1: You said you never were in the States before.
Woman 2: Yes.
Woman 1: Yet you just said you have been here for two years.
Woman 2: No. Two days. I arrived here two days ago.

*She turns to GEORGIA.*

What's the answer?

ROB: I know the answer.

*AMALIA and GEORGIA turn to him.*

The woman is using "America" correctly as the name of the continent from the North to the South Pole is America. The name given to the union of the colonies in the Northern Hemisphere is The United States of America. It's a descriptive name. It was suggested by John Adams and it stayed. The woman was living or traveling in Canada, or any of the Central or South American countries for the last two years.

GEORGIA: It's a descriptive name? You mean they could have called it ... South of Canada.

ROB: Well the Spaniards did that in the Southwest.
A place with mountains, was "Montana."
That means mountain.
A yellow place was "Amarillo."
That means yellow.
A place with snow was "Nevada."
That means snow.
A red place was "Colorado."
That means red.
States that are united
Is United States.
And if they are
in America,
they are of America.

GEORGIA: We called America after an Italian who discovered South
America!!!

AMALIA: The whole continent is America. We are the U.S. of it.

GEORGIA: And the rest?

AMALIA: The rest of the countries have names.

*Reading.*

A German mapmaker
engraved a map of the New World
where Amerigo's discoveries
were outlined.

On it was engraved Amerigo's name
From that
Amerigo's Map.
From that
America.

GEORGIA: When I hear "America,"
I see the star-spangled banner
and the stripes.
I see red, white, and blue.

ROB *gradually becomes distressed by what he reads.* GEORGIA *looks at one of the
maps.*

# Maps

GEORGIA: Look at this.

*Looking more closely.*

Look here.

*Pause.*

There's no Palos.

*GEORGIA looks at the other map.*

Now look at this.

AMALIA: What?

GEORGIA: Look here.

*GEORGIA moves her finger around until she finds what she is looking for.*

Here's Palos.

AMALIA: Ah.

GEORGIA: We're not lost.

AMALIA: What do you mean?

*GEORGIA points to the first map. She slides her finger in the area where Palos should be.*

GEORGIA: Well, in this map there's no Palos.

*Indicating the other.*

But in this one there is a town called Palos. Here it is.

*Pointing.*

Look at these two maps. They are of the same area. Southern Spain. Look at this. They look different. Don't they? Does this look the same as this?

AMALIA: No.

GEORGIA: Do these two look like maps of the same place?

AMALIA: No.

GEORGIA: Look at this map.

*They look at it.*

And look at this one.

*They look at the other. Then, GEORGIA points to the first.*

Look here. See this road here?

*Pointing to the other.*

It's not here.

*Pointing at the same.*

Look at this. This,

*Pointing at the other.*

It's not here. Why is that?

*AMALIA is closely looking at both maps.*

> Things are built, then abandoned,
> then ruined, then destroyed.
> Then rebuilt. A bridge is built.
> It's repaired. Then it collapses.
> A dam is built. The land is razed.
> There's a landfill. A town is built.
> It starts to crumble. This town is abandoned.
> This town prospers. It's beautiful.
> Then, it falls apart. Then it's abandoned.
> Then it's rebuilt. The ashes pile.
> And pile again. Layers. Upon layers
> of ashes pile and pile. There are ashes
> in the air. The air is contaminated.
> The senses atrophy. Fumes disintegrate

brain cells. Common sense atrophies.
We don't recognize ourselves. We can't
see the physical world. Common sense
is replaced by non-ideas expressed by
non-words, and non-gestures.

AMALIA *notices that* ROB *is distressed. He starts walking to the table.*

AMALIA: ... What's the matter?

ROB *sits. He stares.*

    ... Rob ... ?

# Newspapers

ROB: (*Note: He will read a couple of items about war, injustice, violence.
Indicating the newspaper.*) Well ... this.

AMALIA: What ...

ROB: This.
    Children have to fight wars,
    have their little bodies blown apart.
    Women are raped and gorged.
    Why do we do such terrible things?
    The gods look at us
    and we're in a state of shame.
    As we need.
    And need.
    And need!
    Need and need more.
    Need more
    and more
    and more.
    Have more
    and more.
    Not yet enough!
    Not enough!
    Not yet enough!
    Till we bury ourselves
    in garbage,
    pestilence

bitterness
and abuse.

## A drop of water

AMALIA: (*Nervously.*) Where are we in relation to all this?

GEORGIA: Us?

AMALIA: Yes, us here in Spain.
How do these people here see us?
As part of what? As part of that?
Are we a part of that?
How do they see us in relation to all this?
Will they think
we're responsible?
Will they think we're a part of it?

*She stands.*

Are we in danger?
Will someone tear the clothes
off our backs?
Beat us? Spit at us?
Hate us? Tear our limbs off?
Walk on our mutilated bodies?
Will they think we're guilty
of these things?

GEORGIA: Don't worry, Amalia.

AMALIA: … because we're Americans?
Does the world hate us?
Do they blame us for those things?
Does the world hate us?

Are we guilty
of those terrible things?
I don't want to
think we're a part of it.

*She starts to cry and sits.*

People are so unkind
to those who're not
exactly like them.

They beat someone
because he is
of a different race,
because he speaks a different tongue,
because he's poor,
because he loves someone
of his own sex,

because she is of a different sex.
They hate children.
They torture them
and mutilate them.

What is happening to us?
People kill
for a gadget.
They kill
for a pack
of cigarettes.
They kill
just to kill.

*She sits, still breathless.*

I'm not talking about being nice.
Just to know that others exist.
To be curious about others.
To want to know someone other than yourslf.
Not just to be nice,
but to be curious.
"Oh, look at this. Look at that.
Oh, look at that man. What's he doing?"
"Oh, he's picking up something. I wonder
what it is." "Oh, that woman is leaning over.
She's telling him something." "I wonder
what she's saying?" Just that.
You don't have to weep.
Just be curious.
That's how you know other people exist.
If you are not curious, you are alone.
What do you think bliss is?

To go outside yourself. That's all.
If you experience nothing but yourself
you'll feel no relief.
To get lost outside yourself is bliss.
Not always thinking "I, I, I, I." "I enter."
"I exit." "I'm up." "I'm down."
"I wear this." "I wear that." "Do I like this?"
"I don't like that." "I drink."

*She pants as if hyperventilating.*

"How do I look?" "How am I doing?"
"How does this look?"
You go around in circles.
Around and around.
And you lose your balance.
You get crazy and wild
and mean and cruel.
But if
you look outside yourself,
you feel
a natural person.

You see,
and you wonder,
and you feel
another, and you learn

And you love and
that's how you feel
a natural person.

If you think only of yourself
you get crazy and frustrated
and wild and mean and cruel.
That happens to the ones who
are in power
as well as to the ones
who're not.

They also loot and kill and rape.
The same as the ones who are not in power.
They steal and kill
for petty things.
They never think beyond themselves.

What do you think is the reason for cruelty
and oppression
and bigotry
and racism
and a desire
to be drugged
and numbed
and anesthetized.
If God could,
he would

*As she puts her finger in a glass of water.*

come back

*As she lets a drop of water fall on the table and points to it.*

and say,
"Look at this drop of water.
Therein lies
everything."

## Christian mystics

BURT *enters. He stands between* GEORGIA *and* ROB. *He indicates a large circle with his arm. Musical arpeggios accompany his movements, gestures, and words.*

ROB, GEORGIA, *and* AMALIA: (*Covering their noses and gagging in reaction to his bad smell.*) Ugh.

BURT: (*Speaking in an intense and eccentric manner and illustrating his words with gestures.*) Christian mystics saw the earth as a circle. And they saw the moon as her mother.

*He raises his arms. The others gag and cover their noses.*

A great white bird who spends the night

*He opens his legs and pantomimes a large egg coming out of his groin.*

brooding over her egg.

Others saw the earth

*Indicating a large circle with his arms. The others gag and cover their noses.*

as the yolk of an egg.

*He puts his finger in the imaginary egg and licks it. The others gag.*

Yum yum.—

*Lifting his arm. The others gag and cover their noses.*

How does that strike you?

*Lifting his arm. The others gag and cover their noses.*

The air around the earth was the white of the egg.

*Lifting his arm. The others gag and cover their noses.*

The blue above the clouds was the skin inside the shell.

*Indicating a large circle with his arms. The others gag and cover their noses.*

And the fire around it was the shell that binds it.

*He lifts his arm to point to the others.*

How does that strike you?

*Silence.*

No one has any comments? No comments?

*ROB raises his hand. BURT points to him.*

You.

ROB: Is the egg hardboiled or soft boiled?

*They laugh. BURT growls.*

BURT: (*Indignant.*) Some,

*Pointing to each.*

one-two-three-

*He gestures as if throwing something on the floor and presses his foot on it as if crushing a cockroach.*

can't conceive things beyond their noses. Some,

*Pointing to each.*

one-two-three-

*He repeats the above.*

can't even conceive their noses.

*They laugh derisively.*

It's hard boiled. Close to the surface it is. It's hard boiled. Deep inside it isn't. It's soft. Volcanoes. Hot egg yolk.

*He licks his fingers.*

Yum yum.

*He laughs. Then, he speaks to* STEVE.

Don't look at me like that. I can't stand that look. You think I've done something wrong or something? Are you a faggot or something? I bet you he's a faggot. Don't look at me like that. I don't feel right about that. I get a feeling in my stomach, like it's going to turn. It makes me feel like puking.

*He makes sounds as if vomiting all over the floor. The others huddle together, cover their noses and make sounds of protest. He then speaks to* STEVE.

What's the matter with you?

*He mumbles to himself. Then, he speaks to the others.*

I have this plan. It's a thought.

*As he does a karate chop.*

It's like walking through walls.

*As he does a karate chop.*

It's like walking through walls.

*As he does a karate chop.*

It's like walking through walls.

> It's like thinking
> you're walking through walls
> because you know you can.
> It's reality that comes

*He sits on the floor.*

> from the depth of the earth.
> And from the outside.

*Moving the tips of his fingers against each other as if weaving minuscule threads.*

> Like mathematics:
> insignificant signs
> that attest to forces
> not yet known to man,
> but are clear as sound.
> You can go
> through the center of the earth

*He does a backwards shoulder roll.*

and come out the other side.

*Intensely.*

You think I'm crazy?

*Coyly.*

I'm not.

*As he skips to the right.*

I speak symbolically.

*He sits on the floor on the right.*

Others know what I know.
They too are obsessed.
They too feel compelled.
Compelled, like only those
who imagine things,
can be compelled.

We have experienced it
in the mind.
And we must experience it
in reality.
Because we know we can.
That's why we're compelled.

*He turns to* STEVE.

Have you ever experienced that? Hm?

*Pointing to each coyly.*

You? You? You? You?

*He laughs.*

It looks like this.

*He turns his back to the audience and lifts his buttocks with his hand while he lets a Bronx cheer out of his mouth.*

Some don't understand this.

*Standing and turning his back.*

Others understand it and sit on

*He wiggles his buttocks.*

their asses. I won't stop till I put it to work.

I'm a modern man!
No one knows that.
Don't you know that?

*He does a spin down kick.*

I'm a modern man!

*He does a spear hand crescent.*

I'm a modern man!

*He does a spear hand crescent.*

I am
a modern man!

*He does a spear hand crescent. Then he exits talking to himself, laughing, singing, whistling, and doing a Charlie Chaplin walk.*


# The Indies

STEVE: (*With his eyes fixed front.*) As beehives are filled with bees,
the Caribbean Islands
were filled with natives
whom the Spaniards called Indians.
Of any soul that ever existed,
God chose the purest and the noblest
and in one fell swoop,
he placed them there.

Let it be known that because of the Spaniards' insatiable greed and ambition and their desire for riches and for gold and their desire to improve their position in disproportion to their worth, and because the Indians were so humble, patient, and easily subdued; because the Spaniards did not deign to treat them even as they would treat beasts (would that they had treated them as beasts instead of as dung in the public square) because of this, hundreds of thousands died without pity and without faith or holy sacrament.

*Gospel.*

What I'm about to say
is a truth

that everyone even the tyrants
and killers,
know and confess to.
Never,
in all the Indies,
did an Indian
cause any harm
to a Christian.

Instead they thought
they came from heaven
even though they received
nothing but harm, theft, death,
violence and humiliation
from them.

AMALIA: (*In a whisper. Referring to* STEVE.) Who's that?

GEORGIA *and* ROB *look at* STEVE.

## The church with the steps

AMALIA *looks at her book and reads.*

AMALIA: "May 9th. Train to Burgos.
    Slept there near the station.
    At 7 A.M. went to Vigo.
    From there went to Lisbon,
    Portugal.
    Very beautiful, Lisbon.
    Left Lisbon on Friday
    went on to Cordoba
    got good rooms with three beds each
    and hot water in the bathrooms.
    From there we went through Seville
    on the way to Cadiz
    with the beautiful
    cathedral
    and waterfront promenade
    like Havana."

*To the others.*

Is this right? Are the dates right?

ROB: Yes, they're right.

AMALIA: (*Reading.*) "Then back to Seville. We went to the church with the steps and saw the tall tower and the courtyards with the potted plants hanging on the walls."

ROB: Amalia, you are my sister and I know you're very smart. But is that all you can say about the cathedral in Seville? "The church with the steps?"

AMALIA: Yes.

ROB: Oh, Amalia, Amalia, Amalia.

AMALIA: Where the people dance flamenco and sing like they have their souls in their throats.

*AMALIA does a flamenco intonation. GEORGIA is tickled by this and giggles. In unison, all three make sounds as if giggling and talking while they put on sunglasses, pick up their drinks, cross their legs and drink while they continue making sounds of laughter and fake animated conversation—as children imitating sophisticated adults.*

## The red hat

*GEORGIA puts down her drink.*

GEORGIA: This morning I went out
     looking for the store
     where I saw the red hat
     and I got lost.

          I went this way
          and that way
          but I couldn't remember

     where I was.

     So I walked up to a man and I said,

          Puede ayudarme?
          I am lost.
          Estoy partida.

Puede ayudarme
Estoy partida. Partida.

And he smiled and said,

Mmm mmm mmm mmm
Mm Mm
Mm mm Mm mm mm.

So I went to a woman and said,

Puede ayudarme?
I am lost.
Estoy partida.

Puede ayudarme
Estoy partida. Partida

And she looked worried and said,

Mmm mmm mmm mmm
Mm Mm
Mm mm Mm mm mm.

Then, I came upon a man in a café and I said,

Puede ayudarme
Estoy partida. Partida.

And he offered me his glass and said, "Drink red wine. It will help you."
And I said, "I don't need red wine. I'm already partida. Tell me where's
that store. Estoy

Partida.
Partida.

And he said, "Red wine will ease the pain." I am partida but I have no
pain. Why won't they show me the way?

ROB: You said, "I'm broken." Lost is "perdida."

*They laugh.*

GEORGIA: Oh, well. Then. I just walked and walked. Hopeless … discouraged.
Walked and walked.
When suddenly.
I was standing
In front
of the store
With-the-Red-Hat!
In front of the store
with-the-Red-Hat!

And how was your day?

AMALIA: I lost my passport, but then I found it.
And—I got a date—
for tonight.

GEORGIA and ROB: What!

*Clapping.*

With whom?—With whom?

AMALIA: With-the-clerk-in-our-hotel!

GEORGIA: (*Clapping.*) He's cute! He's cute!

AMALIA: And he found my passport! I left it on the counter! And I gave him
a kiss!

*To ROB.*

And what did you do today?

ROB: I did fine.

GEORGIA: What did you do?

ROB: I was looking
for shoe polish.

GEORGIA: Shoe polish?

ROB: To shine my shoes.

AMALIA: And?

ROB: I said "shoe polish"
                    and no one understood.
                              I said
                                      "Shoe polish?"
        And no one understood.

        Then I went

*Moving his arms as if holding the end of a rag on each hand to polish a shoe.*

        like this,
                and someone said,
                          "Maracas!"

GEORGIA and AMALIA: (*Disappointed.*) Oooh ...

ROB: Then someone said,
        "Betún."
        And that was right!

*He lifts a foot and points to the polished shoe.*

        Betún!

*This is a kind of "bee bop."*

AMALIA and GEORGIA: Betún, betún,
        Betún-betún-betún.

ROB: Be-bebe Be-be
        Be-bebe Be
        Be-be-be Bebe
        Be-be-be Tún.

GEORGIA: So that's how you say shoe polish ...

ROB: (*Pointing to his shoe.*) Sure. Betún.

*To GEORGIA.*

        So. Did you buy the hat?

GEORGIA: I bought it.

AMALIA: Where is it?

GEORGIA: (*As she goes to where she has hidden it.*) I bought it. I bought it. I bought it.

*As she puts on the hat.*

The red hat!

ROB: The red hat.

AMALIA: The red red hat.

GEORGIA: Hat, hat, hat.

ROB: (*As GEORGIA returns to the table.*) The red hat.

ROB and AMALIA: The red red hat.

GEORGIA: (*As she sits.*) Hat, hat, hat.

ALL THREE: The red, red hat.
    Hat, hat, hat.

    Hat hat.

*In unison, all three put on sunglasses, cross their legs, and pick up their drinks while they make sounds imitating animated and sophisticated conversation as children do and miming laughing and drinking.*

## A malady

ROB: This coffee's terrible. Whose idea was it to come to this place?

AMALIA: I don't know whose idea it was.

ROB: From now on I'm taking charge of the travel plans.

AMALIA: You're not taking charge of the travel plans. You're terrible at making plans.

ROB: Of all places you had to choose this?

AMALIA: (*To Rob.*) You always have to blame someone else when things go
wrong.

> You always do.
> In your life,
> you always blame
> someone not you.
>
> When something
> goes wrong.
> You blame anyone
> but yourself.
>
> You manage to find
> someone to lead you.
> So you can blame
> someone not yourself
> if something
> goes wrong.
>
> So you can feel
> superior and oppressed
> at the same time.
> And pout and
> lose spirit.
> And feel obedient
> and rebellious
> at the same time.
> And righteous and
> ineffectual
> at the same time.
> How can you manage all that?
> How can you manage to be righteous
> an ineffectual at the same time?

ROB: It's a defect of my generation.

AMALIA: Well, quit it.

ROB: Can't help it. It's there and it's going to stay. So forget it.

AMALIA: You're stupid!

ROB: That's right and I can't help that either. And you're more stupid. And
you don't even know it.

GEORGIA: You're both stupid. So quit it.

AMALIA: You quit it! He just must blame someone else for everything that goes wrong.

ROB: Whom have I blamed?

GEORGIA: A malady in his mind and in the minds of so many, many, many, many, many.

AMALIA: It's a malady.

GEORGIA: Blaming other people.

ROB: I haven't blamed anyone.

GEORGIA: Something is not right. So we think someone else is responsible.

AMALIA: Never us.

GEORGIA: No one is responsible.

AMALIA: It's always them.

GEORGIA: Whoever appears to be responsible.

AMALIA: Whoever is in charge.

GEORGIA: When you make someone else responsible for your own life ...

AMALIA: That's how the world ends.

GEORGIA: It just dies.

AMALIA: Simply.

GEORGIA: Simply.

## Socializing

BURT: (*Entering.*) That's nice. Very nice. It sounds nice.

*He sits on GEORGIA's lap and puts a piece of candy in front of her.*

Candy for you.

*He puts another piece of candy in front of* AMALIA.

And this is for you. You don't have to thank me.

*To* GEORGIA.

My father had a tavern.

*Pointing his finger to* GEORGIA's *head like a gun.*

And yours? What does your father do?

GEORGIA: He's an accountant. Why?

BURT: (*Crossing his arms and pointing the fingers of his other hand at* AMALIA.) And yours? What does your father do?

AMALIA: Why do you want to know?

BURT: To hold him up. Ha ha ha ha ha ha. I want to hold up your father.

*To* GEORGIA.

And your father too. Bang bang.

*He laughs and snorts. Then, to* AMALIA.

Bang bang.

*He laughs and snorts. Then blows on both fingers like guns.*

I'm being sociable.

*He laughs.*

AMALIA: That's not a way to be sociable.

BURT: I'm not talking to you. I'm talking to her. When I talk to you I'll be sociable to you.

*He makes sounds of pleasure as he moves his eyebrows.*

Now I'm being sociable to her.

*He makes sounds suggesting friendly conversation.*

You ask me how is one sociable? You ask the person what their father does. You tell the person what your father does. And you get to know each other. Socialize. You want to know what my father does?

GEORGIA: (*Pushing him off her lap.*) I don't care what your father does. You want to socialize? Socialize with someone else. Don't socialize with me.

BURT: Why not madam? I'm a gentleman and I think you're cute.

*To AMALIA.*

You're cute, too. Yum yum.

*He licks his lips. Then, to both.*

I was married once to a nice woman. Nice family. Nice house. Solid middle class. But it didn't mean anything.

GEORGIA: It didn't?

BURT: (*Standing.*) Not a thing. Except I had a son. One can have a son very easily.

*Thrusting his pelvis forward.*

Hump. Hump.

*Pulling his pelvis back.*

If you pull out two seconds before, you don't have a son.

*Thrusting his pelvis forward.*

If you don't pull out you have a son. Having a son takes two seconds.

*Thrusting his pelvis forward twice.*

Hump-Hump. You can have a son in two seconds.

*Pulling his pelvis back.*

If you pull out two seconds before, you don't have a son.
There are people who believe the Earth is square.

*They all laugh loudly.*

Ancient Peruvians did. The Aztecs thought the universe was in the shape
of five squares.

*Pantomiming five squares around GEORGIA's head.*

One in the center and one extending from each side.

*They all laugh loudly.*

Some have seen the Earth as a wheel.

*They all laugh.*

And so on and so on. What do we think now? Or do we think? Think …
think. They said I went crazy because I started seeing mermaids. What's
wrong with that?

*He becomes agitated and speaks rapidly.*

It's better than seeing people who want to destroy you and want to take
advantage of you. Better than seeing people take everything from you.
Everything that you worked for day and night every day of your life.

*Starting to pull at his leg.*

It's better to see your leg rot while it's still attached than to see it cut off.
Better to see it gangrene and give you pain worse than you ever imagined
than to let it be taken off … because it's yours.

*He starts to walk down of the table.*

just like those islands were mine. They said I saw mermaids. I didn't see
mermaids. I said I saw mermaids. Because I saw something that resembled
mermaids.

*He sits on his haunches and emulates the sensuality of the manatee.*

Round faces, big eyes, long eyelashes. Sensual bodies with breasts like women. When a man sees a manatee he can get a hard on. They're something like seals, only a lot more attractive. A lot more human. It still turns me on to think of them. Round shoulders like girls. Round breasts. Soft skin. Like mermaids.

*He starts going upstage and up the slope.*

They said I lied. I didn't lie. It was partly lies and partly ignorance. What does that make me? Good? Bad?

*To* STEVE.

You have something against me?

STEVE: I have nothing against you.

BURT: (*Continues going up.*) You have nothing against me because I cut the hands of Indians? I didn't. Didn't you know that? They were laughing at me.

*He falls to the floor and convulses as if with an epileptic attack.*

I didn't! I didn't! I didn't!

AMALIA: What's wrong with him?

## The holy fathers in the desert

STEVE: The Spaniards came into the lands of the Indians and they saw the Indians as ravenous wolves and tigers and lions. Since their arrival all they did was mangle them and butcher them and impale them, and dismember them, and torture them and drive them to despair and inflict upon them every imaginable form of cruelty that man has ever suffered from man. Because of their cruelty, those islands were despoiled and left desolate. Christians started by taking the Indian women and children to serve themselves and to misuse them. They ate the Indian's food which was the fruit of their sweat and toil. Because they wanted more than what the Indians gave them of their own free will (what was enough meat for three Indian families of ten for a month, a Christian ate in one day). Because of these and other ills perpetrated, Indians started to understand that those men could not have come from heaven. Indians were clean and had clear and quick minds. They were capable and docile and were open to any good teaching that was taught to them. Of all people the Indians possessed the least amount of material goods and had little desire to possess more. They were not ambitious, not greedy. They were not presumptuous. Their food was so plain, the Holy Fathers in the desert could not have eaten more plainly. Except for a loincloth, they walked in the nude. They slept on a simple mat on the floor, or sometimes on a net that hung from trees. The Christians overpowered them. The Indians' weapons were too weak to defend them against the Spaniards' horses, spades and lances and such cruelty as they had never known.

## The bottom of the well

BURT: In the town of Syene
      in the Greek colony of Egypt,
      on the first day of summer

*Pointing upward with the pointer.*

      at exactly noon,
      the sun shines
      exactly overhead.
      Now, on that day at noon,

*He places the bottle on the floor.*

      if you look down the deepest well,

*He puts his eye to the mouth of the bottle.*

      you will see the sun
      shining on the bottom
      of the well.
      In the third century A.D.
      Eratosthenes knew this.
      And listen
      to what he did.
      He looked
      for the tallest tower

*Placing the stool at a distance from the bottle. He taps the bottle with the tip of the pointer and draws a line to the tower.*

following the straightest line due North from the well, 517 miles north of Syene, was Alexandria. On the first day of summer, at exactly noon, when the sun was hitting the bottom of the well in Syene, in Alexandria the tower threw a shadow of 7.5 degrees, which is 1/48th of the 360 degrees in a circle. Eratosthenes multiplied the distance between Alexandria and Syene by 48 to complete the circle and arrived at 24,816 for the miles of the Earth's circumference, which is only 50 miles off the actual measurement of the Earth's circumference through the poles. In the third century A.D. they not only knew the Earth was round but they knew the measure of its circumference.

*Expecting a reaction.*

What do you think of that?

*Wielding his pointer.*

You're not impressed? You think you could've figured it out? Never!

*He growls.*

You think you could've?

*He throws the pointer on the floor and walks away.*

## The shrouded ship

*The shrouded sailboat crosses the stage. The black cloth is now tattered. The ship is filled with garbage bags.*

## Sailing

STEVE: (*Setting himself as the mast of the boat. He illustrates what he describes.*)
  The front part of the boat
  is the bow,
  and the back is the stern.
  "Abeam" means
  to either side of the boat.
  If I am the boat
  then things are
  in relation to me.
  The right side of the boat
  is called
  the starboard side.
  The left side is called
  the port side.

On a sailing boat,
let's say a sloop,
there is one mast.
My neck and my head
are the mast.
And this arm,
is attached to the mast,
and it's called the boom.
Now the main sail is a triangle
formed from the top of the mast
coming down to the end of the boom
and running along my arm.

Sloops have another sail
attached to the top of the mast
called a jib or a foresail.
Now it can run free on either
side of the mainsail.
So, here we have two sails;
a mainsail and a foresail.
I'm sailing and I want to get to

*Indicating the direction of the house.*

that house over there.
The wind is coming

*Indicating to the same direction as the house.*

from that direction.
I can't sail directly to the house
because that would be sailing
into the wind.
What would happen is my sails
wouldn't fill.
They'd "luff."
Which is like a rustle and shake
and the boat doesn't move.
So, what I have to do
is zigzag, or tack
towards that house.

*Pointing.*

There's the house.

To do that
I steer a little
off from the direction
of the wind.
My sails will fill and I'll begin to move
and I would be on a starboard tack
because the wind is
coming over
the starboard beam
of the boat.
Then, after a while
I have to zag or
"come about"
which is changing
to the other tack.
Now I steer the boat
to starboard
and the sails
come across
and fill this way.
The wind is coming over
the port beam
of the boat,
and we're now on a port tack.
After a while
I have to zag or
"come about" again
and now we're on
our way
tacking towards the house.
There's also something
called "a reach"
where the wind comes from off of
either beam.
The wind is abeam.
Now the sails can be let out
a little further,
but not too much.
If you let the sails out
too far they'd luff again.
The sails still have to be
pulled in order to catch the wind.
Now, the big maneuver is
"running free" where the wind

is behind you—either directly
aft or only slightly off the aft.
Here the sails can really be
run out
because the wind's pushing directly
and going just where we want to go.
You could have one sail on each
side which is called "wing in wing"
where the mainsail and
foresail are over either beam.
But that's rarely done.
If the wind's fluky
or very strong
you can't do that.
Now, if you're "running free"
and you need to change direction,
you have to "jibe"
and that's a lot trickier
than "coming about."
Because what that means is,
you have to bring the stern
through the wind.
And you have to really know what
you're doing
because if you don't
and the wind is very strong
you can either capsize the boat,
or the boom can come across
with such force
that it can rip the boat apart.

BURT: (*To* GEORGIA *and* AMALIA.) See? You thought it was easy? It's not that easy.


# In perpetuity

BURT: The land where you're standing is mine, in perpetuity. How could I
not be fit to govern what is mine in perpetuity. They owe me ten percent
of all the profits from all the lands I own and still own and will own in
perpetuity, by contract which I hold.

*He takes an old stained piece of paper from his pocket. He shows it to* GEORGIA.

Here it is. In perpetuity.

*To AMALIA.*

See? In perpetuity. See it was a business. A business enterprise. I was supposed to get ten percent in perpetuity. Like a patent. It was supposed to be a business ... like any other. But it was too big. So I was left out.

*To ROB.*

See? In perpetuity.

*He puts the paper in his pocket.*

## Conga Line

BURT: (*Taking GEORGIA by the hand.*) Okay. Come, let me show you around. Have fun.

GEORGIA: (*As she goes with him.*) Why?

BURT: I've been around. Get it? Round?

*As he starts doing a conga step.*

Tata tatata ta. Ta ta tatata ta.

GEORGIA: (*To AMALIA. As she joins BURT in the conga step.*) You wanna come?

AMALIA: (*To GEORGIA.*) You're going?

GEORGIA: Yeah.

AMALIA: Why?

GEORGIA: It may be fun.

BURT: I've been around. Get it?

AMALIA: (*Joining the conga line.*) Okay.

*To ROB.*

You're coming, Robbie?

*ROB shakes his head.*

Ciao.

*They exit singing.*

Ta-ta Ta-ta Ta Tá
Ta-ta Ta-ta Ta Tá.

GEORGIA: Ciao.

BURT: Ciao.

## Crystal ball

*ROB goes towards the café. He stops and turns to STEVE.*

ROB: Would you like some coffee?

STEVE: No, thanks.

*ROB takes a few more steps and turns to STEVE again.*

ROB: Would you like anything else?

*STEVE looks at ROB.*

Soda?

STEVE: Yes, please.

ROB: I'll get it.

*ROB exits. STEVE goes to the table and sits down. ROB enters with a bottle of soda and gives it to STEVE. STEVE lifts the bottle to offer a toast and drinks. ROB sits across from STEVE and watches him drink. Then, he stands and walks a few steps to the left.*

ROB: When I was seven I lived in fear of a tall skinny boy who was crazy. I was afraid of him and he knew it. When he saw me in the street he came to terrorize me. I'd continue walking but he'd catch up with me and tap me on the shoulder. I would become paralyzed and break into a cold sweat. He would reach for my pencil box and take whatever he wanted as he said strange things in a strange voice. When he finished he threw the box at me and walked away whistling. I've tried to protect myself against being wounded or humiliated by anyone.

*ROB is despondent and puts his head down. A car enters on the stage left area. GEORGIA is at the wheel. AMALIA noticing that ROB is upset comes out of the car and takes a few steps towards him.*

AMALIA: ... Rob ... let's go ... .

*ROB moves to the table.*

... It's time to go ... .

*Pause.*

What's the matter?

ROB: (*Speaking in a very intense manner, with his eyes blank, as if in a trance.*) If you look into a crystal ball and ask, "Crystal ball, will there be such a thing as the end of the world?"

*Short pause.*

The crystal ball doesn't answer ... Why don't you answer, crystal ball?— Will there be such a thing as the end of the world?

*To AMALIA.*

It doesn't answer. Do you know?

*There is a moment's silence.*

ROB: Why don't you answer?

*To STEVE.*

Is this the end of the world?

*Pause.*

Why don't you answer?

*AMALIA tries to help ROB up.*

# Christians

STEVE: Christians slapped them, punched them and beat them with sticks and even raised their hands to the chiefs.

*AMALIA and ROB take a couple of steps left. ROB turns to STEVE violently as AMALIA tries to restrain him and pull him away.*

ROB: (*Swinging his arm towards STEVE.*) Shut up! Shut up! Shut up!

*AMALIA pulls him towards the car. ROB speaks over STEVE's lines.*

Shut up! Shut up! Shut up!

*AMALIA forces ROB into the car and gets in herself. The car starts moving slowly.*

STEVE: They entered the town and without sparing either children or elders or pregnant women or new mothers, they tore them to pieces as if they were sheep in their flock. They made bets that with one slash of their knife, they could disembowel and rip a man in half, cut off his head, or cut open his belly. They took infants from their mother's breast and by their feet flung them against boulders. They threw them in the river and pushed them under, shouting, "Float whoever you are." They put a sword through both the infant and the mother and anyone else whom they found in their path. They hung 13 men close together in a bunch with their feet just touching the ground. And, in the name of our redeemer and the 12 apostles, they lit a fire under their feet and burned them alive. Others were wrapped in dry straw and were set on fire. Others had their hands slashed and with their hands still dangling from their wrists they were sent walking into the hills where rebel Indians were hiding. They trained fierce dogs to tear the Indians to pieces and eat them as if they were pigs. They tied Indians and put them on a grill to roast under slow burning embers.

*The car appears in the promontory. AMALIA and GEORGIA get off the car and walk to the edge to listen to STEVE. ROB follows. He stands next to GEORGIA. Soon he starts to sob.*

While they screamed in pain, their souls left them. Once the Indians screamed so loudly that the Captain, either because he felt sorry for them or because the screaming kept him from sleeping, he ordered that they not be burned but drowned. The guard did not drown them, instead he put sticks in their mouths to make them silent. He kindled the fire and let them roast even more slowly while he waited.

*GEORGIA has put her arms around ROB. She starts to lead him back to the car. AMALIA follows. Saetas are heard in the distance.*

I saw all the things that I have said and even more. I know the name of the guard and even his relatives in Seville.

*The car starts. The lights begin to fade slowly all around STEVE.*

Because once in a great while, though ever so rarely, an Indian did kill a Christian, they passed a law that for every Christian killed, Christians could kill one hundred of them.

*The last light begins to fade as the volume of the music increases and is heard through the actors' bows.*

# Manual for a Desperate Crossing

DEDICATED TO HORACIO,
AND TO THOUSANDS OF MEN, WOMEN, AND CHILDREN WHO
PERISHED CROSSING THE FLORIDA STRAITS ON RICKETY RAFTS.

From conversations with:

José Abreu
Ibis Amigo
Reinaldo Alfonso
Angel Cancelo
Sunset Cancelo
David Cartaya
Armando Castillo
Evelyn Crusata
Guillermo Delgado
Lázaro Díaz
Nadia Díaz
Frank Enrique
Francisco Escobar

Federico Falcón
Armando Ferrer
Agustín García
Ernesto González
Nancy Lledes
Dámaso Pérez
Braulio Quevedo
Jorge del Río
Rafael Rodas
Johanka Ródriguez
Ariel Ruíz
Dulce María Trejo
Ernesto Wong

*Manual for a Desperate Crossing (Balseros/Rafters)* premiered at the Florida Grand Opera, Colony Theater, Miami Beach, Florida, on May 16, 1997. It was commissioned and produced by the Florida Grand Opera, Miami-Dade Community College, Wolfson Campus, and South Florida Composers Alliance.

*ASHLEY ENSEMBLE ARTISTS*
Sam Ashley
Thomas Buckner
Thomas Hamilton

Jacqueline Humbert
Joan La Barbara

*FLORIDA GRAND OPERA YOUNG ARTIST STUDIO MEMBERS*
Demetra Adams
Emmanuel Cadet
Christina Clark

David Dillard
Amy Van Roekel

*ACTORS*
Nattacha Amador

Mario Salas-Lanz

Maria Irene Fornes, *Libretto*

Robert Ashley, *Composer/Conductor*

Michael Montel, *Stage Director*

Charles R. Caine, *Costume Designer*

Jorge Alberto Fernández,
*Set and Lighting Designer*

*MUSICIANS*
Oseiku Da-El Díaz

Oscar Salas

# CHARACTERS

BALSERO 1: Youngest, in his 20s. Capable, well built, experienced in rafts and sailing. Gentle and unassuming.

BALSERO 2: Middle, in his 30s. Thoughtful and responsible. Good natured. Arranges and provides. Stocky. A widower with a four year-old daughter.

BALSERO 3: Oldest, late 40s. Stocky, not very bright, cares and worries about everyone, overzealous.

BALSERO 4: Middle. Capable, well-built, experienced in boats and sailing.

BALSERA A: Youngest. Good looking, cheerful.

BALSERA B: Middle. Intelligent, practical, physically strong, a sense of humor.

BALSERA C: Oldest. Married to BALSERO 3. Very much like him.

CHORUS

*A scrim on the back wall and sides will permit projections of films or slides with titles (a smaller screen) or additional scenery (slides of film) using the total area of the back wall and sides (a calm or stormy ocean, a beach).*

*On each downstage side and on the back corners there are giant papier-mâché waves that resemble Japanese engravings in style.*

*Against the back wall center there is a platform with as many taburete chairs as there are actors. When they are not performing they will sit there.*

*Downstage center there is the main platform. About two feet from the edge of this platform there is a railing. On the back, front, and sides of the railing there are entrances. Along the upstage side of the platform there is a step about ten by ten feet and the width of the platform. On the downstage side of the platform there is another step about ten by ten feet and the width of the platform that leads to the stage floor level. On the upstage side of the raft there is a platform approximately six by six feet and about eight inches higher than the upstage step. There is also a railing around this platform with openings on the sides. To the right and left sides of the raft there are the upper parts of the oars (as many as there are performers minus one) which are not visible until they are lifted up and are attached in such a way as to move like oars pushing against water. The platform will have the capacity for different levels of oscillating motion. In the center of the platform there is a slit that will hold a keel. On the platform is a living room set: two armchairs and one or two rocking chairs of black mahogany with black caning and a small table with a crochet doily, a couple of framed portraits, a small black vase with painted flowers, paper flowers, and a paper pad and pencil. Against the side walls there are as many short stools as there are performers. Against a wall there is a cardboard box that contains the parts for a distillery mentioned in the text. A stick and a rag will be concealed behind the platform or by the stools. The Spanish text will be projected on the screen.*

## 1. En un bote de remos   On a Small Boat

*B*ALSERO *2 is sitting on the rocking chair to the right. B*ALSERA *B is sitting on the rocking chair to the left.*

*Image 1: Stop-and-go frames of a film. An immense ocean. The camera begins to close in on a rowboat. The waves become larger and larger.*

*The lights on the platform begin to come up.*
*The scene starts.*
*The film continues through the following and goes into Image 2.*

B*ALSERO* 1

| | |
|---|---|
| Si sales al mar | If you go out to sea |
| en un bote de remos | on a rowboat |
| sientes pánico. | you are frightened. |
| | |
| En mar abierto | Out at sea |
| la embarcación | the vessel |
| es frágil. | is frail. |
| | |
| En una tormenta | In a storm, |
| una | one |
| sola | single |
| ola | wave |
| la destruye. | can destroy it. |

*Image 2: A stop-and-go film. The storm sets in. It envelops and overpowers the boat. Pieces of the boat fly off. The film continues through the following and goes into Image 3.*

## 2. En un lago            On a Lake

*Image 3: Stop-and-go close-up film of an oar pushing gently against calm waters. The camera zooms out gradually showing more of the boat, then the lake. The film continues through the following scene.*

BALSERO 3

| | |
|---|---|
| En un lago, no. | Not in a lake. |
| En un lago | In a lake |
| el remo | the oar |
| se impone. | prevails. |
| El agua | The water |
| se le entrega. | yields. |
| | |
| En un lago, | In a lake, |
| el remo, | the oar, |
| aunque chico, | small as it is, |
| domina. | commands. |
| | |
| El agua cede, | The water gives in, |
| lo recibe. | It yields. |
| | |
| En mar abierto, no. | Not out at sea. |
| | |
| En mar abierto— | Out at sea— |
| el remo | the oar |
| se rinde. | surrenders. |
| Se dobla, | It bends, |
| se somete. | submits. |
| | |
| La barca está | The boat is |
| a la merced | at the mercy |
| del viento | of the wind |
| y del mar. | and the sea. |

*The film fades off.*

# 3. El riesgo      The Risk

*All but BALSERO 2 stand in the back in a line.*

BALSERO 2

| | |
|---|---|
| El que se echa a la mar | He, who goes out to sea |
| en balsa | on a raft |
| arriesga su vida. | risks his life. |
| Y la vida | And the life |
| de sus hijos, | of his children, |
| de su esposa. | of his wife. |

| | |
|---|---|
| De su madre, | Of his mother, |
| su hermana, | his sister, |
| su amigo, | his friend, |
| su vecino. | his neighbor. |

| | |
|---|---|
| De aquel que se lanza. | Of those who chance it. |

| | |
|---|---|
| Algunos salen y regresan. | Some set out and return. |

| | |
|---|---|
| Cuando sienten el poder | When they feel the power |
| del mar | of the sea |
| regresan. | they return. |

| | |
|---|---|
| Después que salen, | After leaving, |
| alguien dice, | someone says, |

*Those in the back echo* BALSERO *2's gestures and words.*

| | |
|---|---|
| "No voy." | "I'm not going." |
| "Yo no voy." | "Not going." |
| "Regreso." | "I'm going back." |
| "No sigo." | "I won't go." |
| "Yo regreso." | "I'm going back." |
| "No sé nadar." | "I can't swim." |
| "Es muy duro." | "It's too hard." |

*He points to an imaginary child, hands open. The others, standing in the back, repeat his gestures and echo his words.*

| | |
|---|---|
| "No sabe nadar." | "She can't swim." |
| "La niña | "The kid |
| no sabe nadar." | can't swim." |
| Y regresan. | They return. |
| Soñó | He dreamt |
| irse del país | of leaving the country |
| y no pudo. | and couldn't. |

| | |
|---|---|
| A veces | Sometimes, |
| quien | he who |
| fabrica | builds |
| la balsa | the raft, |
| sale. | goes out. |
| Y es él | And it's he |
| quien | who |
| quiere | wants |
| volver. | to return. |

| | |
|---|---|
| Quien luchó tanto | He, who worked hard |
| por hacer la balsa, | to make the raft, |
| sale, | leaves, |
| y después dice, | and then says, |
| "Sigan ustedes, | "You go on, |
| yo no voy. | I'm not going. |
| No puedo." | I can't." |

| | |
|---|---|
| Regresa | He returns |
| la balsa | the raft |
| a la playa | to the beach. |

| | |
|---|---|
| Ya habían salido, | They had already left, |
| y los hizo | but he made them |
| volver. | go back. |

*Indicating to the imaginary child with open hands.*

| | |
|---|---|
| "La niña." | "The kid." |

*He looks at them, hoping they will understand.*

| | |
|---|---|
| "No puedo." | "I can't." |
| "Sigan ustedes." | "You go on." |
| "Déjenme en la playa." | "Leave me on the beach." |
| "Ven, corazón." | "Come, sweetheart." |

*He is despondent, stretches his hand towards the child. His hand closes as if holding her hand. He speaks to imaginary people on the raft.*

| | |
|---|---|
| "Buena suerte." | "Good luck ... to you." |

*He waves, turns and walks up with his arm outstretched as if holding the child.*

## 4. Planes y arreglos

## Plans and Arrangements

*Image 4: The same subject as Image 1 (closing in on a rowboat, waves getting larger) filmed from a different angle. It starts out-of-focus and very slowly goes into focus through the following scene.*

*In "B's house." BALSERO 1 is sitting on the armchair to the right. BALSERA B is sitting on the armchair to the left. The doorbell rings.*

BALSERA B
    Alguien toca.

Someone knocks.

*BALSERA B walks towards the upright area.*

BALSERO 1
    Estoy en casa de amigos.
    Alguien toca.

I'm in a friend's house.
Someone knocks.

*BALSERA A enters.*

BALSERA B
    Una vecina.

A neighbor.

*Image 5: On stage: B and A walk to center. B points both hands towards A, then towards 1. A and 1 bow. B offers A the rocking chair to the left. They both sit. There is a moment's silence.*

*B turns to look at A.*
*A turns to look at 1.*
*B turns to look at 1.*
*1 turns to look at A.*
*B turns to look at A.*

*Image 6: On stage: A walks to B's side. A leans over and puts a key in B's hand.*

BALSERA A
*In a whisper.*
    Toma esta llave.

Take this key.

*Closing B's hand.*

| Mañana, | Tomorrow, |
| toca mi puerta. | knock on my door. |

*Gesturing.*

| Tun tun. | Knock knock. |

*She puts her ear to an imaginary door.*

| Si no abro, | If I don't answer, |
| es que me fui. | it means I left. |

| Abre con la llave, | Use the key, |
| entra, | go in, |
| y toma lo que quieras. | and take what you want. |

| Si no estoy, | If I'm not in, |
| es que me fui. | it means I'm gone. |

BALSERO 1

| Por muchas vías | From many sources |
| oíamos | we heard |
| que muchos | many |
| salían | were leaving |
| en botes | on boats |
| y balsas. | and rafts. |

*Image 7: Film of rafters navigating a river with a current.*

*Image 8: On stage, there is a knock on the door. BALSERA B is starting to go to the door as BALSEROS 2, 3, and BALSERA C enter and stand in a group. BALSERO 1 looks at his watch.*

BALSERO 1

| A las dos | Others arrive |
| llegan otros. | at two. |

*Image 9: On stage, through the following sequence, each addresses the person who just spoke.*

BALSERA B
Buenas noches.

BALSERA C
*To B.*
Buenas noches.

BALSERA B
*To 2.*
  Buenas noches.

BALSERA 2
*To B.*
  Buenas noches.

BALSERA B
*To 3.*
  Buenas noches.

BALSERO 3
*To B.*
  Buenas noches.

*2, 3, and C walk towards the platform, stand in a group and turn to A.*

BALSERA A
*To C.*
  Buenas noches.

BALSERA C
*To A.*
  Buenas noches.

BALSERA A
*To 2.*
  Buenas noches.

BALSERA 2
*To A.*
  Buenas noches.

BALSERA A
*To 3.*
  Buenas noches.

BALSERA 3
*To A.*
  Buenas noches.

BALSERO 1
*To C.*
  Buenas noches.

*2, 3, and C walk towards 1 and stand in a group.*

BALSERA C
*To 1.*
  Buenas noches.

BALSERO 1
*To 2.*
  Buenas noches.

BALSERO 2
*To 1.*
  Buenas noches.

BALSERO 3
*To 1.*
  Buenas noches.

BALSERO B
  Siéntense.

*BALSERO 1 stands. BALSERA C sits. BALSERO 1 indicates BALSERA A to sit.*

BALSERA C
| | |
|---|---|
| Queremos hacer una balsa. | We want to make a raft. |
| Tenemos los materiales— | we have the materials— |
| pero no | but don't know |
| sabemos hacerla. | how to make it. |

BALSERO 1
*To the audience.*
| | |
|---|---|
| Yo | I |
| me crié | grew up |
| en puerto de mar. | in a seaport. |
| Y de niño | And from childhood |
| ya sabía | I knew how |
| hacer balsas. | to make rafts. |
| Y sabía | I could |
| navegarlas | navigate them |
| con remo | with sail |
| y vela, | and oar, |
| en tormentas | in storms |
| y mal tiempo. | and rough weather. |

*Image 10: Now the waters have turned to rapids in the film.*

BALSERO 1

Después,
me hice geógrafo.
Y fuí asignado
a
territorios
en zonas montañosas
donde corrían ríos
violentos.

Later,
I became a geographer.
And was assigned
to
areas with
high mountains
where wild rivers
flow.

Balsero 1
Ahí hice balsas
y logré navegar
los rápidos.

There I made rafts
and navigated them
in the rapids.

Aquí quieren mi ayuda

Here they want my help.

Lo haré.

I will help.

## 5. Bin-ban

## Bin-ban

BALSERA B
*From the rocking chair.*
De la costa norte
se puede salir
en balsa.
La corriente
te ayuda.
De la costa sur, no.

From the North shore
you can leave
on a raft.
The current
helps you.
In the South, it doesn't.

En la costa sur
la corriente
te lo impide.
Tú remas y remas
y ella te lo impide.

In the South
the current
pulls you back.
You row
and it pulls you back.

De mi pueblo,
en el sur,
ir al norte
en balsa,
no se puede.

From my town,
in the South,
you can't go
North
on a raft.

Y tampoco se puede
en bote, ni de remos

Nor can you go
on a row boat

ni de vela.
La corriente
te hala
y te hala.

or a sailboat.
The current
pulls you back
again and again.

Nunca te atrevas
en balsa.

Never try it
on a raft.

Tienes—que ir
en bote—con motor
Por eso en mi pueblo
se inventó el bin-ban.

You have—to go
on a boat—with a motor.
That's why in my town
we invented the bin-ban.

Si señor, El bin-ban.

Yes, Sir, The bin-ban.

*Image 11: On film, an animated drawing illustrates the tearing down of the inside walls, the boat inside the house, the knocking down of the house's façade, the pulling of the boat to the coast, the launching, the bin-ban cemetery and the sailing.*

BALSEROS 2 AND 3

El bin-ban
es un barco
hecho
de planchas
de automóviles
viejos
atornilladas
y soldadas.

The bin-ban
is a boat
made
from old metal
of old
cars
bolted down
and soldered.

Un barco
fuerte.

A strong
boat.

Al hacerlos
se oye
bin-ban,
bin-ban.

When they're made
you hear
bin-ban,
bin-ban.

El martilleo.

The hammering.

Bin-ban.

Bin-ban.

Y por eso
así se llama
Bin-ban.

And that's why
they're called
Bin-ban.

BALSERA A
  ¿Oh?                    Oh?

BALSERA B
  Bin-Ban.              Bin-Ban.
  El bin-ban se hace   The bin-ban is made
  dentro de la casa.    inside the house.

BALSERA C
  ¿ ... dentro?        ... inside?

BALSERA B
  De la casa.        The house.

BALSERA B
  Se derrumban     They knock
  las paredes       the inside walls
  interiores        of the house
  de la casa.        down.

BALSERO 2
  De veras ...       Really ...

BALSERA B
  Sí.               Yes.
  Y allí           And there
  se hacen        they make
  los bin-banes.    the bin-bans.

  En la casa       Inside the
  desmantelada    gutted house
  no hay          there're
  paredes.         no walls.

  No hay          There's
  mas             only
  que un barco.     a boat.

BALSERO 1
*(Showing her the drawing.)*
  ¿Así?             Like this?

BALSERA B
  Así.             Yes.
  Cuando llega el momento When the moment comes

se derrumba
la fachada
y se saca
el barco.

the front wall
goes
and the boat's
hauled out.

Algunos
lograron
salir.
Otros no.

Some
managed
to leave.
Others not.

En el puerto
había
un cementerío
de bin-banes
confiscados.

In the port
there was
a cemetery
of confiscated
bin-bans.

## 6. La balsa

## The Raft

BALSERO 1
Este es el diseño
de la balsa.

This is the design
for the raft.

*Image 12: On film, a diagram shows the details, as BALSERO 1 describes them. An arrow moves from place to place, to indicate the parts already drawn.*

*Image 13: On stage, BALSERO 1 stands. From a distance, he uses a pointer to indicate the figures as they appear on the screen.*

BALSERO 1
Plataforma
de madera.
Mástil.
Quilla grande.
Y timón.

Platform
of wood.
Mast.
A big keel.
And a helm.

Sin paredes.
Así el agua
entra y sale.

No sides.
So the water
comes and goes.

Abajo
dos o más
cámaras
y bloques
de poliespuma.

Underneath
two or more
innertubes
and blocks
of polyurethane.

Todo se cubre
con malla
gruesa de nylon.

All is covered
with thick
nylon net.

Si hay tormenta
recogemos la vela
y vamos al timón.
Y si no, a los remos.
Un amigo de mi primo
es carpintero de ribera.

In a storm
we gather the sail
and move to the helm.
And if not, to the oars.
A friend of my cousin's
is a shipyard carpenter.

BALSERO 1
    Nos puede ayudar.

    He'll help.

Lo haremos
en el patio.

We'll make it
in the yard.

## 7. Materiales
## Modos y formas

## Materials
## Ways and Means

*Image 14: On stage, they take the furniture off the platform, bring in a keel, a mast, a sail, oars, and a school-chair top. One ties a piece of fabric to the mast. They put the keel through the slit on the platform, set the oars, the mast, the sail, the helm, as they mention the parts.*

BALSERO 1
Tenían
cámaras,
poliespuma,
madera,
tornillos,
y taladros.
Faltaba lona
y resinas para pegar.
Nos dimos a la tarea
de robarnos lona
de almacén militar.

They had
innertubes,
polyurethane,
wood,
screws,
and drill bits.
We needed canvas
and resins for gluing.
We set out on the task
of stealing the canvas
from the army warehouse.

El guardia,
un recluta,
amigo de mi amigo,
nos dejó
entrar
el camión
al patio.

The guard,
a recruit,
friend of a friend,
let us
bring
the truck
in the yard.

Por cien pesos
rompimos la puerta
y sacamos
tres pacas de lona
que se usa
para cubrir
tanques de guerra.

For 100 pesos
we broke a door
and took
three bundles of canvas
that's used
to cover
war tanks.

BALSERO 3
La nuestra
quedó
rústica.

Ours
was
crude.

No muy bien
pensada.

Not too well
thought out.

Llevaba armazón
de hierro.
Pensamos que
la haría fuerte.
—Inexperiencia—
—Resultó pesada. —

It had an
iron frame.
We thought it'd
make it strong.
—Inexperience—
—It was heavy. —

*He holds the school-chair top.*

El timón
era la tabilla
de una silla de escuela.
Como esta.

The helm
was the board
of a school chair.
Like this.

Tenía quilla.
Tres cámaras:
una de Volvo,
dos de camión.
Forradas
con malla de nylon
y lona.
Un mástil,
vela,
y remos

It had a keel.
Three tires:
one a Volvo,
two from a truck.
We covered them
with nylon net
and canvas.
A mast,
sail,
and oars.

BALSERO 1
El primer día
nos robamos la lona.
El segundo y tercero
armamos la balsa.

The first day
we stole the canvas.
The second and third
we built the raft.

En el cuarto
pegamos
las planchas de poliespuma.
Y las presionamos
con tornillos.
Le hicimos
un dobladillo
a la lona.
Y la clavamos
al marco de madera.
Quedó fuerte.

On the fourth
we glued
the sheets of polyurethane.
And we tightened them
with screws.
We made
a hem
on the canvas.
And nailed it
to the wooden frame.
It was strong.

## 8. Empacando      Packing

*Image 15: On film, a close-up of a man (stop-and-go) standing in the water. He arranges and ties bundles to a raft.*

*Image 16: On stage, those on stage do a dance in unison. The movements have a ritual/work or exercise quality.*

BALSERO 2
    Ya por salir,      About to leave,
    bien atados los paquetes:      the bundles tightly packed:

*All touch the fingers on the left hand with the right index as if counting.*

    Alimentos, medicinas      Food, medicines,
    agua, gasolina,      water, gas, special
    instrumentos especiales:      instruments:

*Making a fist with the right hand and bringing the fingers up one at a time.*

    Brújula, fósforos,      Compass, matches,
    termómetro, aguja, cuchilla,      thermometer, needle, knife,

*Touching the small finger of the left hand with the index of the right.*

    hilo esterilizado      sterilized thread
    (para heridas).      (for wounds).
    Para el mareo:      For seasickness:

*Touching the second finger of the left hand with the index of the right.*

    Inyecciones intramusculares.      Intramuscular injections.
    También      Also
    sales orales      oral salts
    para la      for
    desidratación.      dehydration.
    Lápiz, papel, pluma.      Pencil, paper, pen.

# 9. Otros ayudan          Others Help

*Image 17: The blurred close up of a woman's face slowly starts to move into focus during the following. She has long thick black hair. She wears a long-sleeve black dress.*

BALSERO 2

| | |
|---|---|
| Cada cual en su puesto, | Each to his spot, |
| su lugar. | his place. |
| Su cuerda | His rope |
| para atarse | to be tied |
| al dormir | when going to sleep |
| por si hay mal tiempo. | in case of bad weather. |
| Para no caer al mar. | Not to fall into the sea. |
| Sombrero para cubrirse | A hat to shield from |
| del sol, | the sun, |
| camisa de manga larga. | long-sleeve shirt. |
| Algo impermeable | Something waterproof |
| por si llueve. | in case it rains. |
| Algo de abrigo | Something warm |
| para el frío | for the cold |
| de la noche. | of the night. |

*Image 18: The face is now in focus. The mouth is wide open. She is calling. A wind instrument does the sound of her voice.*

BALSERO 2

| | |
|---|---|
| Ya estamos todos. | We're already |
| en la balsa | all on the raft |
| Yo parado en el agua. | I'm standing on the water. |
| La empujo. | I push it. |
| Voy a subir. | I'm about to jump up. |
| | |
| Oigo una voz. | I hear a voice. |
| Alguien llama. | Someone calls. |
| Me viro. | I turn. |

*Image 19: On film, a woman is running down the beach. She holds a shoebox high in the air. She calls.*

BALSERO 2

| | |
|---|---|
| Una señora viene corriendo. | A woman comes running. |
| ¡Esperen! ¡Esperen! | Wait! Wait! |
| Trae una caja. | She holds |
| Chica, | a small box. |

de zapatos.
Corre,
esperamos.

shoe box.
She runs,
we wait.

Me entrega la caja.
… Se mueve.
Dice,
"Es una paloma.
Cuando lleguen
la sueltan.
Ellas vuelven.
Saben volver …
a su hogar …
Así sabré
que están bien.

She hands me the box.
… It moves.
She says,
"It's a pigeon.
When you reach land,
let it go.
They return.
They know how …
to come home …
It'll tell me
you're safe.

Si no,
no volverá."
Dice.

If not,
she won't return."
She says.

Se preocupa.

She's worried.

Otra señora
corre.
Nos regala
su sombrilla.
Y dice,

Another lady
runs.
Gives us
her umbrella.
And says,

"Para el sol"

"For the sun."

# 10. En la Balsa

# On the Raft

BALSERO 3
La hicimos
en un día.
De prisa,
y nos fuimos;

We made it
in one day.
Rushed it,
and left;

*They all count with their fingers.*

mi esposa,
mi sobrino,
un vecino,
mis dos hijos,

my wife,
my nephew,
a neighbor,
my two sons,

| mi hija, | my daughter, |
| yo. | myself. |

*Image 20: On stage: all but BALSERO 3 drop seated on the raft, making a clean stumping sound.*

BALSERO 3
*Counting seven fingers.*

| Siete. | Seven. |
| | |
| En una balsa. | In one raft. |
| Y salimos. | And left. |

*Image 21: As the raft begins to move slightly, BALSERO 3 makes a complete circle, staring at the distance.*

| Ya saliendo | Going out, |
| conté | I counted |
| treinta | thirty |
| balsas | rafts |
| a la vista. | in view. |
| | |
| Felices. | Happy. |
| Como en día | Like a day |
| de regata. | of regatta. |

*The stage starts to darken.*

| Mientras tanto, | In the meantime |
| del Norte | from the North, |
| viene | the storm is |
| la tormenta. | nearing. |
| Y— | And— |
| hacia ella | to it |
| sin remedio | unavoidably |
| | |
| la corriente | the current |
| nos lleva. | is driving us. |
| | |
| Ella | The storm |
| hacia nosotros | towards us |
| y nosotros | and we |
| hacia ella. | towards the storm. |

| Quinta Parte | Fifth Part |
|---|---|
| *la noche negra* | *the black night* |

## 11. La tormenta

## The Storm

BALSERO 3 AND CHORUS

El cielo
se ve gris
Y el viento
está agitando
el mar.

The sky's
gray.
And the sea's
getting
rough.

*The movement of the raft starts to increase.*

*Image 22: On film, through the following, an ocean in turmoil is projected all over the stage. Powerful fans blow on their hair, clothes, and fabric on the mast. There is the sound of a roaring ocean.*

A cada lado
los muchachos
reman.

On each side
The boys
are rowing.

Y reman y reman
y el oleaje aumenta.

They row and row.
And the surge increases.

Y reman.
Aumenta.

They row.
It increases.

Reman.
Y
aumenta.

And they row.
And it
increases.

*Image 23: On stage, they hold on to each other, make throwing up sounds and roll on the floor as the ocean throws them.*

Una ola alza la balsa
y la arroja
contra el agua.

A wave lifts up the raft
and slams it
against the water.

La alza de nuevo
y la tira de nuevo.

Up again and
it slams down again.

La levanta
y la arroja
contra el agua

It lifts it up
and it hurls it
against the water.

Y sube
y la
lanza
contra
el agua
otra vez.

And up
and it's
hurled
against
the water
again.

Y una vez más
la balsa
se alza.
Y
cae
de nuevo.

And again
the raft
goes up.
And
down
again.

Está a la merced
de las olas.

It's at the mercy
of the waves.

El viento
sopla
y golpea
los ojos.

The wind
blows
and it beats
on our eyes.

Y golpéa
los oídos,
y la piel.

And it beats
on our ears,
and our skin.

El viento
golpéa
y golpéa.

The wind
beats
and beats.

Y golpéa
la cabeza.

And it beats
on our heads.

BALSERO 3 AND CHORUS
Y el viento
golpéa
los nervios.

And the wind
beats
on our nerves.

*Image 24: There is the sound of an explosion. The raft jerks violently. They let out a scream.*

| | |
|---|---|
| ¡Aaah! ¡Una cámara se poncha! | Aaah! A tire bursts! |
| ¡No resistió el peso! | Couldn't bear the weight! |
| ¡No-resistió-el-peso! | Couldn't-bear-the-weight! |
| | |
| ¡Ni los golpes! | And the pounding! |
| ¡Ni los golpes! | And the pounding! |
| | |
| ¡Y se poncha! | It blows up! |
| ¡Y se poncha! | It blows up! |
| ¡Nos hundimos! | We're sinking! |
| ¡Nos hundimos! | We're sinking! |
| ¡Ay! ¡Nos hundimos! | Oh! We're sinking! |
| ¡Nos hundimos! | We're sinking! |
| ¡Nos hundimos! | We're sinking! |

*Image 25: On stage, they are hysterical. Their voices are shrill. They move according to what they describe.*

| | |
|---|---|
| ¡Pánico! | Panic! |
| ¡Agárrense! | Hold on! |
| ¡Arrástrense! | Crawl! |
| ¡Al centro! | To the center! |
| | |
| ¡Agárrense! | Hold on! |
| ¡Agárrense! | Hold on! |

*Image 26: There is the sound of a helicopter propeller while a searchlight scans the stage. BALSERO 1 starts to make a torch with a stick and a rag.*

| | |
|---|---|
| ¡Aparece un helicóptero! | A helicopter appears! |
| ¡Un helicóptero da vueltas en el aire! | A helicopter circles above us! |
| ¡Anda buscando Balseros! | It's looking for rafters! |
| ¡Anda buscando Balseros! | It's looking for rafters! |
| Balseros desamparados en la oscuridad. | For helpless rafters in the dark. |
| ¡Nos busca! | It's looking for us! |
| ¡Nos busca! | It's looking for us! |
| ¡Nos busca! | It's looking for us! |

| | |
|---|---|
| ¡Aquí estamos!!! | Here we aaare!!! |
| ¡Aquí estamos! | Here we aaa aa a a aa are! |
| ¡Aquí estamos! | Here we aaa aa a a aa are! |

BALSERO 3

| | |
|---|---|
| Mi—hijo—empieza | My—son—starts |
| a hacer—una—antorcha. | to—make—a—torch. |
| De prisa. | In a hurry. |

CHORUS
*To the helicopter.*

| | |
|---|---|
| ¡Aquí estamos! | Here we aaaare! |
| ¡Aquí estamos! | Here we aa aa re! |
| ¿No nos ven? | Can't yo-uu see us? |

*Image 27: On stage, making figure eights, looking at the floor.*

BALSERO 3 AND CHORUS

| | |
|---|---|
| Buscamos los fósforos. | We look for matches. |
| ¡Busca los fósforos! | Look for matches! |

*They all stamp on the floor at a given interval as they're making figure eights looking at the floor for the matches.*

BALSERO 3 AND CHORUS

| | |
|---|---|
| Buscamos los fósforos. | We look for the matches. |
| ¡Busquen los fósforos! | Look for the matches! |
| ¡Para la antorcha! | To light the torch! |
| ¡Para la antorcha! | To light the torch! |

*Image 28: On stage, they stand still and feel their pockets as they sob, cry, and wail. They continue the stamping.*

| | |
|---|---|
| ¡No están aqui! | They're not here! |
| ¡No están aqui! | They're not here! |
| | |
| ¡Aquí no! | Not here! |
| ¡Aquí no! | Not here! |
| | |
| ¿Donde están? | Where are the matches? |
| ¿Donde están? | Where are the matches? |

*They raise their hands to their heads in despair.*

| | |
|---|---|
| ¡Se han caído al mar! | They fell in the water! |

| | |
|---|---|
| ¡Se han caído al mar! | They fell in the water! |
| ¡Se han—caído—al mar! | They—fell—in the wat—er! |
| Los—fósforos—se han caído | The matches are not here— |
| Tienen que haber caído | They must have fallen in the |
| a l a g u a !!! | w a t e r !!! |
| | |
| Aaaahhhhh!!! | |
| Los—fósforos—se—han— | The—matches—have fallen— |
| caído—al mar! | in—the—water! |

*They stamp on the floor.*

Aaaahhhhh!!!

*Image 29: On stage, they all drop to the floor and beat on the floor with their fists.*

BALSERO 3 AND CHORUS
Aaaahhhhh!!!

| | |
|---|---|
| … No tenemos fósforos!!! | … We have no matches!!! |
| ¿Donde están? | Where are they? |
| ¿Donde están? | Where are they? |

*They raise their hands to their heads in despair.*

| | |
|---|---|
| No podemos encender la antorcha. | We can't light the torch! |
| No podemos encender la antorcha. | We can't light the torch! |

*They pull their hair.*

| | |
|---|---|
| ¡Se han—caído—al mar!! | They—fell—in the water!! |
| ¡¡¡Se han—caído—al mar!!! | They—fell—in the water!!! |
| | |
| ¡No nos ve! | They can't see us! |
| ¡No nos ve! | They can't see us! |
| El helicóptero | The helicopter |
| no nos ve. | can't see us. |

*Looking for the matches so feebly disconcerted.*

| | |
|---|---|
| ¿Donde están? | Where—are—the matches? |
| ¿Donde están? | Where—are—the matches? |

*Image 30: They raise their hands and arms slowly in despair. Then they start squirming and convulsing on the floor.*

| | |
|---|---|
| Se han caído al mar! | They fell in the water! |
| Al—mar!! | In—the—sea!! |
| Se han caído al mar!!! | They fell in the sea!!! |

*There is a pause.*

| | |
|---|---|
| Se va—el helicóptero. | The helicopter—is leaving. |
| Se—va. | It's—leaving. |
| Sin—vemos. | Didn't—see uuus. |
| | |
| Se fué | It's gone |
| Se—ha—ido | It—is—gonnne. |
| Nos ... | It ... |
| ha ... | has ... |
| dejá ... | left ... |
| do ... | us ... |
| a | to |

```
a                           d
 ho                          r
  gar                         o
   n                           w
    os                          n


      e                           i
       n                           n


        l                           d
         a                           a
                                      r
          o                           k
           b                           n
            s                           e
             u                           s
              r                           s
               i                           .
                d
                 a                          .
                 d
                                            .

                                            .
```

*They sing a song without words, which is composed of crying, sobbing, whimpering, and wailing.*

*Sound: Then, there is the sound of the water against the raft. The crying begins to subside and the sound of the water on the raft is more audible. Then, in addition, the sound of rowing and the murmur of voices approaching are heard.*

*Image 31: They shift to face upstage. They put their hand to their ear and listen. While the sound of rowing and the murmur of voices increases in volume, on their knees and elbows, they take two quick steps upstage in unison—stop—turn their heads to one side, put their hand to their ear and listen and turn their heads upstage to look. Then, they repeat the action to the other side. Then, they turn upstage again, take two quick steps (on knees) upstage and the complete sequence is repeated several times.*

*Image 32: On film, people clustered on a raft. The camera closes in on their faces. There is the sound of waves beating on the boat.*

BALSERA B AND CHORUS

| | |
|---|---|
| Aparece una balsa | A raft appears |
| ¡Se acerca! | It comes closer! |
| ¡Se acerca más! | And closer! |
| | |
| ¡Se acerca! | Closer! |
| ¡Se acerca más! | And closer! |
| ¡Se acerca! | Closer! |
| | |
| ¡Se acerca más! | And closer! |
| ¡Se acerca! | It comes closer! |
| ¡Se acerca más! | And closer! |
| ¡Se acerca! | Closer! |
| ¡Ofrecen ayuda!! | They—offer—help!! |
| ¡Sí! ¡Sí! | Yes! Yes! |
| Nos ayudan. | They will help. |
| | |
| ¡Sí! ¡Sí! ¡Sí! | Yes! Yes! Yes! |
| ¡Gracias! ¡Sí! | Thank you! Yes! |
| ¡Sí! ¡Sí! ¡Sí! | Yes! Yes! Yes! |
| ¡Sííí! | Yeees! |
| | |
| ¡Sí! ¡Sí! ¡Sí! | Yes! Yes! Yes! |
| ¡Sí! ¡Sí! ¡Sí! | Yes! Yes! Yes! |
| | |
| ¡Gracias! ¡Sí! | Thank you! Yes! |
| ¡Sí! ¡Sí! ¡Sí! | Yes! Yes! Yes! |
| ¡Sííí! | Yeees! |

¡Sí! ¡Sí! ¡Sí!            Yes! Yes! Yes!
¡Gracias! ¡Sí!            Thank you! Yes!
¡Sí! ¡Sí! ¡Sí!            Yes! Yes! Yes!
¡Sííí!                    Yeeees!

*Image 33: On film, "The boys jumping in the water and tying the two rafts together."*

*On stage: BALSEROS 1 and 2 roll off the raft upstage.*

BALSERA B AND CHORUS
Se hechan al mar          The boys jump
los muchachos,            in the water,
y atan                    and tie
las dos balsas.           the rafts together.
¡Y estamos a salvo!       We're saved!
¡Salvos y sanos!          Safe and sound!
¡Salvos y sanos!          Safe and sound!
¡Salvos! ¡Salvos! ¡Salvos!  Safe! Safe! Safe!

*Image 34: The boys join the rest. They arrange themselves to lie down close together to be farther away from the edge. BALSERO 3 sits apart.*

BALSERO 3
Buena gente.              Good people.
Arriesgaron              They risked
su vida                   their lives
por nosotros.             for us.

En total somos            In total we're
quince                    fifteen
y dos niños.              and two children.
Demasiados.               Too many.
Y aún así                And yet,
vienen                    they came
y nos rescatan.           and rescued us.
¡y nos rescatan!          and rescued us!
¡¡y nos rescatan!!        and rescued us!!
¡¡¡y nos rescatan!!!      and rescued us!!!
¡¡¡Buena!!! ¡¡¡Gente!!!   Good people!!!

*Image 35: On stage, they all jump and stir simultaneously as if by a rough wave. Some lean over the edge and throw up. They return to a position of rest. BALSERO 3 is still sitting.*

| | |
|---|---|
| Nosotros, cansados. | We, tired. |
| ¡Pero a salvo! | But safe! |
| Algunos | Some |
| con mareo | seasick |
| y vomitando. | and throwing up. |
| | |
| Yo, cansado, | I, tired, |
| nervioso, | nervous, |
| agotado, | exhausted, |
| vigilo. | keep watch. |
| Otros descansan. | Others rest. |
| Yo no. | I don't. |
| | |
| Me preocupa | I worry |
| que alguien | someone |
| se descuide | may get careless |
| y caiga al mar. | and fall in. |
| | |
| O que se le caiga un | Or let an arm drop |
| brazo al agua | in the water |
| | |
| y un tiburón | And let a shark |
| se lo arranque. | tear it off. |
| | |
| Un padre se preocupa. | A father worries. |
| ¡Hay razón!! | With reason!! |
| Se preocupa. | With reason. |

*They turn to their side and snore.*

| | |
|---|---|
| z z z z z z z z | z z z z z z z z |
| | |
| Se preocupa ... | A father worries ... |
| Con razón ... | With reason ... |
| se preocupa ... | he worries ... |

*Despondent.*

| | |
|---|---|
| Por eso me preocupo. | That's why I worry. |

*There is a sudden increase in the sound of the storm and the movement of the raft.*

*Image 36: On film, a stormy ocean. A 15-foot boat is moving towards the camera. It is misty and raining.*

*Image 37: On stage, the storm starts increasing in force. As they sing the snoring song they start inching towards the upstage step. They try to advance by crawling, walking on their knees, on all fours, by placing one knee on the floor with their hands, then, the foot of the other leg, then, falling as they are trying to place the foot of the first leg on the floor and falling. When they reach the step, they either lean on it, lie on it, or sit on it. BALSERA B and BALSERO 4 are center.*

*Image 38: On film, at the same time the camera closes in on a group standing close together on the prow of the boat. Their faces are indistinguishable in the dark. They could be the same as those on the raft. They are similar positions to those in the raft.*

CHORUS
*Their boo-hoos are strong, like cursing.*
   Buu!! Juu!                 Boo!! Hoo!

   Es difícil ponerse de pie.     It's difficult to stand.

| | |
|---|---|
| *Sexta Parte* | *Sixth Part* |
| *pasada la tormenta* | *after the storm* |

## 12. Al pairo

## Adrift

BALSERA B

| | |
|---|---|
| Buu!! Juu! | Boo!! Hoo! |

*The storm starts to subside. The movement of the raft begins to decrease and the lights begin to get brighter.*

| | |
|---|---|
| Ya viene la calma. | It's calming down. |
| Pero no estamos mejor. | But it isn't any better. |
| El motor se ha roto | Our motor broke down |
| y la brújula también. | and also did the compass. |

CHORUS

*Their boo-hoos are strong, like cursing.*

| | |
|---|---|
| Buu!! Juu! | Boo!! Hoo! |

| | |
|---|---|
| Perdidos, | We were lost |
| a la deriva, | Adrift, |
| sin agua, | without water, |
| y sin alimentos. | without food. |
| Muertos | Dying |
| de hambre | of hunger |
| y de sed. | and thirst. |
| Ya | Already |
| el sol | the sun |
| secó la | dried |
| boca. | the mouth. |
| Ya quema | It burns |
| la boca | the mouth. |
| ya | It's |
| seca. | dry. |

*They try to breath and fan their mouths with their hands.*

| | |
|---|---|
| Buu!! Juu! | Boo!! Hoo! |
| La piel | The skin |
| quemanda. | burning. |
| La boca | The mouth |
| ardiendo. | in flames. |

| | |
|---|---|
| Deshidratados, | Dehydrated, |
| debilitados, | feeble, |
| ya sin poder | not able |
| estar | to stand |
| de pie | on our feet |
| por cansancio | from exhaustion, |
| habre y sed. | hunger, thirst. |
| Agua en todas partes | Water all around |
| pero no para beber. | and yet none to drink. |
| Agua, | Water, |
| agua, | water, |
| por dondequiera, | all around, |
| y ni una gota | and not a drop |
| para beber. | to drink. |

*They cough.*

| | |
|---|---|
| Sed, sed, | Thirst, thirst. |
| la garganta seca | The throat dry. |
| sin alimento | No food |
| para nutrir | to feed |
| las carnes | the flesh |
| que | which |
| se despegan | starts to hang |
| de | off |
| los huesos. | the bones. |

| | |
|---|---|
| Al pairo!! | Adrift!! |
| A donde nos lleve. | Going where the currents |
| la corriente. | take us. |
| … Perdidos … en … | … Lost … in … |
| el … golfo … | the … Gulf … |
| flotando … | aimlessly … |
| sin rumbo … | floating. |
| Sin agua … | No water … |
| ni alimento … | no food … |

| | |
|---|---|
| Esperando la muerte … | Waiting to die … |
| en las aguas | in the waters … |
| del golfo. | of the Gulf. |

| | |
|---|---|
| Buu! … Juuu! | Boooh! Hoooh! |

| | |
|---|---|
| Sin poder | Not able |
| tenernos | to stand |

de pie.      on our feet.
Agua …      Water …

*They drop to the floor.*

Agua …      Water …

*They open their mouths wide and try to breathe.*

El aire      The air
quema      burns
al respirar.      to breathe.

Agua …      Water …

Agua …      Water …

## 13. Un barco pasa      A Passing Ship

*Image 39: On stage, they start crawling on hands and knees and lifting themselves up to scan the sky.*

CHORUS
Siempre buscando      Forever looking
aves      for birds
en el cielo.      in the sky.
Indicio de      A sign
tierra      we may be
cercana.      nearing land.

*They are now all facing upstage.*

Buscando      Looking
en el horizonte      in the horizon
un contorno      for the shape
de tierra.      of land.

*Image 40: A small cutout of a freighter starts to travel from right to left across the line of the horizon. A musical version of a ship's engine is heard. They put their hands against their foreheads as visors.*

¿Que es eso?      What is that?
Se ve algo en      We see something
la distancia.      in the distance.

| | |
|---|---|
| Algo ... Sí! | Something ... Yes! |
| Un barco! | A ship! |
| Un barco! | A ship! |
| Un barco | A ship |
| en la distancia! | in the distance! |
| ¡Rápido! | Quickly! |

*Image 41: Some start banging on the floor, hitting metal pipes, screaming, and making any other sound they can make as others follow the movement of the ship with their heads and torso.*

| | |
|---|---|
| ¡Hacemos alboroto! | We make noises! |
| ¡Llamamos! | We call! |
| ¡Gritamos! | Scream! |
| ¡Socorro! | Help! |
| ¡Auxilio! | Help! |

*They all look at the ship and make sad murmuring sounds of prayer and hope as the ship starts to disappear.*

Ahhhhhhhhhhh.
Ahhhhhhhhhhhhhh.

*Image 42: On stage, when the ship disappears they bow their heads disheartened and slowly start taking aimless steps in different directions and drop to the floor again. Balsero 4 goes to the side and brings the box with the parts for the distiller to the side of the platform.*

| | |
|---|---|
| Se fué. | It's gone |
| No nos vio. | It didn't see us. |
| Se ha ido. | It's gone. |
| Este es nuestro fin. | This is our end. |
| Al pairo, | Adrift, |
| sin agua | without water |
| ni alimento. | or food. |
| Moriremos de sed. | We'll die of hunger. |
| Moriremos de hambre. | We'll die of thirst. |
| Nos llegó. | This is it. |
| Nos llegó. | This is it. |
| Nos llegó la hora. | This is it. |

BALSERO 4

| | |
|---|---|
| Calma! Calma! | Calm down! Calm down! |
| ¡Aún no ha llegado el fin! | It's not the end! |

*Through the following, they slowly lie on the floor and cover themselves as if shrouding themselves.*

CHORUS
Llegó el fin.          This is the end.
Llegó el fin.          This is the end.

BALSERO 4
No es el fin! Aún no!    Not the end! Not yet!

CHORUS
Este es el fin.        This is the end.
Este es el fin.        This is the end.

BALSERO 4
No-es-el-fin.       It-is-not-the-end.
No-lo-es.           It-is-not.

CHORUS
Ya morimos.        We're dying.
Ya morimos.        We're dying.

BALSERO 4
!No morimos!       We won't die!
¡Aún no!            Not yet!

CHORUS
Sí, sí, sí morimos!    Yes, yes, we'll die!
Ya lo estoy!       We're already dead!

BALSERO 4
No lo estás!       You are not!
No lo estás!       You are not!

CHORUS
Ya morimos.        We're dying.
Ya morimos.        We're dying.

BALSERO 4
¡Les digo que no!    I tell you you're not!

CHORUS
Muertos ya!        Dead, dead!

*They drop their heads.*

ZZZZZZZZZ       ZZZZZZZZZ

## Septima parte
*sobreviviendo*

## Seventh part
*surviving*

## 14. Destilando el agua    Distilling the Water

BALSERO 4
*Banging on pipes.*

| | |
|---|---|
| ¡Despiértense! | Wake up! |
| ¡Hay que hacer | We have to make |
| un destilador! | a distiller! |
| ¡Un destilador! | A distiller! |
| ¡Un destilador! | A distiller! |
| ¡Un destilador! | A distiller! |

*They wake up.*

CHORUS

| | |
|---|---|
| ¿Cómo? | How? |
| ¿Qué? | What? |
| ¿Cómo? | How? |
| ¿Cómo? | How? |
| ¿Qué? | What? |
| | |
| ¿Qué? | What? |
| ¿Cómo? | How? |
| ¿Qué? | What? |
| ¿Ahh? | Ah? |
| ¿Hm? | Hm? |
| Mmm … | Mmm … |

BALSERO 4

| | |
|---|---|
| ¡Despierten! | Wake up! |

*They shake their heads and open their eyes.*

| | |
|---|---|
| Vamos | We're going |
| a tomar | to distill |
| el agua. | sea water. |
| Vamos | We're going |
| a tomar | to drink |
| agua de mar | distilled |
| destilada! | sea water! |

CHORUS
*Each starts speaking the following at the same time but on a different line, creating a loop. When they reach the end, they start again at the top until they have said all the lines.*

| | |
|---|---|
| Nooo. | Nooo. |
| No se puede tomar agua salada. | We can't drink sea water. |
| Nos morimos si la tomamos. | We can die if we do. |
| El agua de mar no | Sea water won't quench |
| sacia la sed. | the thirst. |
| Te da más sed. | It makes you thirstier. |
| Nos dará más sed. | It'll make us thirstier. |
| Te deshidrata. | It dehydrates you. |
| Nos deshidratará. | It'll dehydrate you. |
| ¿Entiendes? | You hear? |
| Nos morimos. | We'll die. |

BALSERO 4

| | |
|---|---|
| Shhhh … | Shhhh … |
| Cálmense… | Calm down … |
| Haremos un destilador … | We'll make a distiller … |

CHORUS
*More quietly.*

| | |
|---|---|
| ¿Cómo vamos a hacer un destilador? | How are we going to make a distiller? |

BALSERO 4

| | |
|---|---|
| Así | Like this. |

*Image 43: On film, the words "Diagram for a distiller" appear written in long hand.*

*Image 44: On stage, each performer takes a part of the distiller from the box and brings it to the upstage platform. As BALSERO 4 is naming each part, it appears in place in the film, and the performer holding the part follows the instruction described.*

BALSERO 4

| | |
|---|---|
| Le amarramos un cordel | We tie a string |
| a la lata | to the can |
| que tiene | that has |
| la tapa de rosca. | the screw-top. |
| | |
| La tiramos | We throw it |
| al agua | in the water |

y dejamos que
la lata se llene.
Le quitamos el serpentín
al motor roto.
Y sellamos
un extremo
a la boca de rosca
de la lata
del agua.

and let
the can fill up.
We take the coil
from the broken motor.
And tightly fit
one end
to the screw-top opening
of the can
with the water.

Una lata vacía
nos sirve de fogón.

An empty can
will be the stove.

Cortamos madera
de la parte interior
del barco,
la ponemos en la
lata que sirve de fogón.

We cut wood
from the inside
of the boat,
and put it in the
can which is the stove.

Salpicamos la madera
con petroleo
y la prendemos.
Se enciende.

We douse the wood
with petrol
and light it.
It will burn.

Ponemos la lata
con el agua
sobre la lata
que es el fogón

We place the can
with the water
over the can
which is the stove.

Tomamos el otro extremo
del serpentín
y lo ponemos
en la lata chica.

We take the other end
of the coil
and place it
in the small can.

Cuando el agua hierve
el vapor sube
por el serpentín

When the water boils
the vapor goes up
the coil.

Según sube
se va refrescando.

As it moves
it starts to cool.

Al refrescarse
se torna en agua.

As it cools
it turns to water.

Y empieza

And starts

a caer
gota a gota ...
agua pura ...
Gota a gota.

to drop
drop by drop ...
pure water ...
Drop by drop.

No suficiente
para saciar la sed.
Solo algo
para prolongar
la espera.

Not enough
to quench the thirst.
Only something
to bear
the wait.

*Image 45: On stage, he starts stabbing the raft. The timing of the words will be adjusted to the rhythm of the stabbing (like the singing of the chain-gang prisoner as he wields his pick).*

A veces lloro,
cuando hundo
mi cuchillo
al costado
de nuestra madre generosa
que sufre sus heridas
sin queja.
Hasta cuando ...
Hasta cuando
podrá
sostenernos ... ?
Hasta cuando ...
Hasta cuando
antes que expire
su último aliento,
y se desplome,
y se hunda
—con nosotros,
sus hijos,
en su herido
vientre—
al fondo
del mar,
herida y débil,
por mi propio filo.

Sometimes I cry
when I sink
my knife
on the side
of our generous mother
who suffers her wounds
without complaint.
How long ...
How long
will she be able
To sustain us ... ?
How long ...
How long
before she expires
her last breath,
and collapses,
and sinks
—holding us,
her children,
in her wounded
belly—
to the bottom
of the sea,
wounded and weak,
by my own blade.

Cada vez que
se hundía en ella
por sacar
pedazos de leña

Each time it
dug into her
to cut
pieces for kindle

| de su costado | from her side |
| parecíame | I thought |
| oírla suspirar. | I heard her weep. |
| Pero no. | But no. |
| Nos daba su vida | She gave her life |
| sin protestar. | without complaint. |
| Para llevarnos a salvo. | To carry us to safety. |
| Barca madre … | Mother vessel … |
| Madre barca … | Mother vessel … |
| | |
| Si no nos salvan | If we're not rescued, |
| antes | before |
| que nuestra nave | our vessel |
| perezca | succumbs |
| por el fiero ataque | to the fierce attack |
| de mi propio filo | of my own knife, |
| se hundirá al fondo | she will sink to the depth |
| hecha pedazos | torn to pieces |
| con su cría a cuesta. | still holding her brood. |
| | |
| Moriremos | We will die, |
| si no de sed, | either of thirst |
| ahogados. | or drowned. |

*They all sob for awhile.*

## 15. Un barco en la distancia   A Ship in the Distance

*Image 46: A small cutout of a freighter travels across the line of the horizon from right to left. A musical version of a ship's engine and horn is heard. They put their hands against their foreheads as visors.*

CHORUS

| Se ve algo | We see something |
| en la distancia | in the distance. |
| Algo … Sí! | Something … Yes! |
| Un barco! | A ship! |
| Un barco | A ship |
| en la distancia! | in the distance! |
| ¡Rápido! | Quickly! |

*They start banging on the floor, hitting metal pipes, screaming, and making any other sound they can make.*

| | |
|---|---|
| ¡Hacemos alboroto! | Make noises! |
| ¡Llamamos! | Call! |
| ¡Gritamos! | Scream! |
| !Socorro! | Help! |
| ¡Auxilio! | Help! |

*They turn again and make murmuring sounds of hope and expressions of hope and disappointment as the ship continues to move and disappears.*

Hm
mm Hmm
mm
mm          Hm
mm Hm    mm
              mm                    mm Hm Hm
                     mm      Hm          mm
                        mm          mm

*Image 47: On stage, when the ship exits they bow their heads and slowly start taking aimless steps in different directions.*

CHORUS

| | |
|---|---|
| Se ha ido. | It's gone. |
| Quizás no nos vió. | They didn't see us. |
| Moriremos de sed, | We'll die of thirst, |
| de hambre. | of hunger. |
| De desesperanza. | Of hopelessness. |
| Moriremos. | We will die. |

*Image 48: On stage, they sit. Ten seconds later there is the sound of a drop falling in the can. They do a slow head turn towards the can, walk towards it in unison surrounding it, go on their knees and make mumbling sounds as they shake their heads with pleasure. They start quickly and gradually the volume increases until it becomes euphoric.*

| | |
|---|---|
| ¡Sí! | Yes! |
| ¡El mar!! | The sea!! |
| ¡El mar!!! | The sea!!! |
| ¡Sí! | Yes! |
| ¡El mar nos da agua!!! | The very sea |
| nos da agua!!! | gives us water!!! |

*Image 49: On stage, they turn to the can and wait for three seconds for the next drop. They turn to look at BALSERO 4.*

BALSERO 4

| | |
|---|---|
| Para aliviar | To relieve |
| la sequedad | the dryness |
| de la boca. | of the mouth. |
| El ardor | The burning |
| de la garganta. | of the throat. |

*During the following scenes there is the slow sound of drops falling. The rafters become progressively weaker and desperate.*

## 16. Sesenta barcos    Sixty Ships

*Image 50: On film, at a distance, different large ships, different angles: large freighters, medium-size ships, fishing boats.*

BALSERA C

| | |
|---|---|
| En veintisiete días | In twenty-seven days |
| pasaron | sixty ships |
| sesenta barcos | passed. |
| Y no pararon … | And didn't stop … |
| No detuvieron su marcha. | They didn't stop. |
| … para ver quieres éramos? | … to see who we were? |
| Para ver qué nos pasaba? | To see what was wrong? |
| Si estábamos muertos? | If we were dead? |
| Si se puede salvar un vida. | If a life could be saved. |
| ¿Ellos se preguntaron? | Did they ask themselves? |
| Los que van | Those |
| ahí … | in it … |
| ¿Murieron? | Did they die? |
| ¿Se ahogaron? | Did they drown? |

## 17. Pescando    Fishing

*Image 51: On film, from under water: A shallow lake where plants grow. Leaves float on the surface. Small fish swim around. A hand goes in from above trying to grab a fish. It escapes. Another fish or a group of fish comes to view. The hand grabs one.*

*Image 52: On stage, BALSERA A lies across the raft with her hand on the left side of the raft. She holds a kitchen knife. BALSERA C lies across the raft with her hand in the water to the right.*

CHORUS
*BALSERA C executes the moves as described.*

| | |
|---|---|
| La sombra de un barco | The shadow of a ship |
| a flote | afloat |
| atrae peces. | attracts fish. |
| | |
| Con la mano | With a bare hand |
| cogíamos pescaditos pequeños | a small fish |
| para carnada. | for bait. |
| | |
| Le amarramos | We tie a string |
| un cordel, | around it, |
| le hacemos | give it |
| un piquete | a cut |
| y lo lanzamos | and throw it |
| al mar. | in the water. |
| | |
| La sangre atrae | The blood attracts |
| al pez más grande. | the bigger fish. |
| Cuchillo en mano | Knife in hand |
| esperamos que pase el pez. | we wait for the fish. |
| Se engancha. | Hook it. |
| | |
| Y del mismo golpe | And in one fell swoop |
| se lanza | we hurl it |
| en la barca | on deck. |
| | |
| Después se cocina | Then we cook it |
| pero no mucho. | but not too much. |
| Porque | Because |
| el pez | the fish |
| en su carne | in its meat |
| lleva | has fresh |
| agua dulce. | water. |
| | |
| Y al cocinarlo | And cooking it |
| se seca. | dries it up. |
| | |
| Mas falta | We need |
| nos hace | more |
| el agua del pez | the water of the fish |
| que su carne. | than its meat. |

*Image 53: They all stand in a semi-circle around the sign.*

## 18. Un solo se acerco    Only One Came Near

*Image 54: On film, stop-and-go images. An enormous freighter at the distance comes closer and closer. The perspective is that of people at sea level.*

CHORUS

| | |
|---|---|
| Un barco se aproxima | A ship comes towards us. |
| Por piedad … | Because of pity … |
| o respeto a la vida? | or respect for life? |
| Se aproxima | It comes to us, |
| al fin | finally, |
| un enorme barco | an enorme ship |
| se acercó | comes close to us. |
| y se detiene. | It stops. |
| | |
| Se asoman unos | Some lean over |
| a la borda. | the railing. |
| | |
| Nos miran. | They look at us. |
| | |
| Nos llenamos | We were |
| de alegría. | filled with joy. |
| | |
| Y de pronto. | And suddenly. |

*Pause.*

| | |
|---|---|
| El barco empieza a alejarse | The ship starts moving. |
| | |
| y se pierde | and disappears |
| | |
| en la distancia. | in the distance. |
| | |
| Nos dejaron a morir. | They left us to die. |
| | |
| ¿Porqué vinieron? | Why did they come? |
| Para ver a unos | Just to look at some |
| que van a morir? | who are going to die? |

BALSERA B

| | |
|---|---|
| ¿Por qué se fueron? | Why did they leave? |
| Por | Because |
| indiferencia? | of indifference? |
| | |
| Recibieron | Did they have |

| | |
|---|---|
| órdenes? | orders? |
| Que nos dejaran ahí … | To leave us there … |
| a morir? | to die? |
| | |
| Quiénes eran? | Who were they? |
| | |
| Hoy viven? | Do they live today? |
| | |
| Eran muertos? | Were they dead? |
| | |
| Puede un ser vivo | Can the living |
| abandonar a otros así? | leave them like this? |
| | |
| Verlos | To see them |
| con sus propios ojos | with their own eyes |
| y dejarlos así? | and leave them like this? |
| A morir? | To die? |
| De sed? | Of thirst? |
| De hambre? | Of hunger? |
| Comidos por el sol? | Parched by the sun? |
| | |
| ¿Piensan en nuestros huesos? | Do they think of our bones? |
| Expuestos | Exposed, |
| yacientes | lying on deck |
| como quedaron | the way they were |
| en el momento que llegó la muerte? | In the moment of death? |
| | |
| Huesos al garete? | Bones adrift? |
| | |
| Nos oyen? | Can they hear us? |
| | |
| Oyen nuestros gritos? | Can they hear our screams |
| eternamente? | forever? |

## 19. Remando     Rowing

*Image 55: They walk to their places on the sides of the raft, pull the oars into place and start rowing gently.*

BALSERA C

| | |
|---|---|
| En el mar seis personas | In the sea, six people |
| tienen que pensar como una. | have to think like one. |
| | |
| Al principio se hace difícil. | At first it's difficult. |

| | |
|---|---|
| Cada uno tiene su opinión. | Each person has an opinion. |
| Pero poco a poco<br>todos sus pensamientos<br>se unen<br>en uno. | But gradually,<br>all their thoughts<br>become<br>one. |

CHORUS
| En el mar seis personas<br>tienen que pensar como una. | In the sea, six people<br>must think like one. |
|---|---|
| Al principio se hace difícil. | At first it's difficult. |
| Pero poco a poco<br>los pensamientos<br>se unen. | But gradually,<br>all the thoughts<br>become one. |

*They row for a while humming a sweet melody.*

# 20. Sed          Thirst

CHORUS
*While they row.*

| Vino<br>el sol<br>del medio día. | The scorching<br>noon sun<br>came. |
|---|---|
| Y nosotros,<br>sin agua<br>ni alimento<br>remando y remando<br>contra la corriente. | And we,<br>without water<br>or food,<br>rowed and rowed<br>against the current. |
| El sol del mediodía<br>nos quemaba.<br>Y nosotros,<br>sin agua,<br>ni alimento,<br>remando<br>y remando. | All the noon sun<br>beat upon us.<br>And we,<br>without water<br>or food,<br>rowed<br>and rowed. |

*Image 56: BALSERO 2 suddenly and rapidly crawls across the platform, drops his head over the upstage side of the platform and desperately drinks water. There is the amplified sound of water splashing and his slurping, swallowing, and heavy*

*breathing. He then brings his head on the raft and lies quietly. They have stopped rowing. One person turns to him, then another, then another until they have all turned.*

*BALSERO 1 goes to him and stands by him.*

Horacio
tomó agua salada
y murió.

Horacio
drank sea water
and died.

*He kneels.*

Murió en la balsa ...
Así,
al lado nuestro.

He died on the raft ...
Like this,
close to us.

BALSERO 1 AND CHORUS
En esa
balsa
Horacio
tomó agua salada
y murió

On that
raft
Horacio
drank sea water
and died

al lado nuestro.

at our side.

No comprendía
que por el agua
podría morir.

He didn't understand
because of water
one could die.

La boca le ardía
y pensó,
"Me calmará la sed.
El agua es agua
y me calmará
la sed."

His throat burned
and he thought,
"It'll quench my thirst.
Water is water
and it'll quench
my thirst."

Parecía que descansaba.
Hasta que vimos
que había muerto.

He seemed to be resting.
But then we saw
he had died.

Pensaste
agua es agua
y te calmará
la sed.

You thought
water is water
and it'll quench
your thirst.

Horacio … Horacio …        Horacio … Horacio …

Y así moriste.              That's how you died.

*They all collapse on the floor sobbing. As the sobbing subsides calm music is heard.*

## Octava Parte
*la llegada*

## Eighth Part
*arriving*

## 21. Cayo Hueso

## Key West

*Image 57: A clear blue sky.*

*On stage, the rafters are sitting by the oars. They are turned to face upstage with their hands to their foreheads as visors.*

BALSERO 1 AND CHORUS

| | |
|---|---|
| Así estábamos | That's how it was |
| cuando | when |
| a lo lejos | at a distance |
| vemos tierra. | we see land. |

| | |
|---|---|
| Con las fuerzas | With the strength |
| que nos quedan | we have left |
| remamos hacia la playa. | we row to the beach. |

*All except BALSERO 2 stand to the right and left of the raft as they sing. They bend down as if picking up the raft and moving it to the sand.*

| | |
|---|---|
| Subimos la balsa | We lifted the raft |
| a la arena | to the sand |
| y fuimos a unas señoras | and went to some ladies |
| que estaban en la arena. | who sat on the sand. |

| | |
|---|---|
| "¿Dónde estamos?" | "Where are we?" |
| "En Key West." | "In Key West." |

*Facing front.*

| | |
|---|---|
| Key West. | Key West. |

BALSERO 1
*Taking a piece of paper out of his pocket.*

| | |
|---|---|
| Saco el número | I take out my aunt's |
| de mi tía | number |
| digo, | and I say |
| "¿Teléfono?" | "Telephone?" |
| Apuntan. | They point. |

*They all turn their heads upstage.*

BALSERO 1 AND CHORUS

| | |
|---|---|
| A unos pasos | A few steps away |
| hay teléfono. | is a phone. |

*They go upstage in a group.*

| | |
|---|---|
| Yo llamo a mi familia | I call my family |
| en Hialeah. | in Hialeah. |
| Otro llama la suya | Someone else calls his |
| en Kendall. | in Kendall. |
| Después llamamos | Then we call |
| a la familia | Horacio's |
| de Horacio | family |
| y volvimos a la arena. | and we returned to the sand. |

*They sit at the edge of the platform facing front.*

BALSERO 1

| | |
|---|---|
| Esperamos. | We wait. |
| | |
| Las señoras | The ladies |
| no hicieron | didn't question |
| preguntas. | us. |
| Pero viéndonos | But seeing us |
| cansados | tired |
| y con sed | and thirsty |

*They produce Coca-Cola bottles from under the platform.*

*Image 58: On the back wall a luminous beach with a light green ocean and a light blue-green sky with a subtle eerie feeling in both lights and music starts appearing.*

| | |
|---|---|
| nos ofrecen | offer us |
| Coca Cola | Cokes |
| "Gracias." | "Thank you." |
| "Muy amables." | "That's very nice." |

*They drink, burp, and nod.*

BALSERO 1

| | |
|---|---|
| "Al punto." | "It hits the spot." |

*Turning to the women.*

| | |
|---|---|
| "Gracias." | "Thank you." |
| "Muy amables." | "That's very nice." |

| | |
|---|---|
| Esperamos. | We wait. |

| | |
|---|---|
| Hay momentos en el mar | There are moments at sea |
| que no se puede decir | when you can't tell |
| si ves el cielo o el mar. | If you see the sky or the sea. |

| | |
|---|---|
| El azul del cielo | The blue of the sky |
| no es el azul | is not the blue |
| que se dice azul. | we call blue. |

| | |
|---|---|
| Es un verde azul. | It's a blue green. |
| Que eso solo se ve | You can only see that |
| en la calma del mar. | when the sea is calm. |

| | |
|---|---|
| Es | It's |
| transparente, | transparent, |
| casi blanco | almost white. |
| Blanco-verde. | White-green. |

| | |
|---|---|
| Y es difícil distinguir | And it's difficult to tell |
| entre el cielo y el mar. | between the sky and the sea. |

| | |
|---|---|
| Cuando vienen las olas | When the waves come |
| ese color transparente | that see-through color |
| se va. | is gone. |

| | |
|---|---|
| A Horacio su familia | Horacio's family |
| lo vinieron a buscar. | came for him. |

| | |
|---|---|
| A nosotros | Ours also |
| las nuestras | came |
| nos vinieron a buscar. | for us. |
| La mía de Hialeah, | Mine from Hialeah, |
| a otro de Kendall. | someone else's from Kendall. |
| Y a Horacio su familia | And Horacio's family |
| le hizo un funeral. | arranged for his funeral. |

| | |
|---|---|
| De todos en la balsa | Of all those on the raft |
| Horacio era | Horacio was |
| mi mejor amigo. | my best friend. |

Era él de todos
mi mejor amigo.

He was of all
my best friend.

BALSERO 1 AND CHORUS
No es el azul
que se dice azul.
Que solo se ve
en la calma del mar.

It's not the blue
It's a blue green.
Which can only be seen
in the calm of the sea.

Es un verde
transparente,
casi blanco.
Blanco-verde.

It's
a transparent green,
almost white.
White-green.

Y es difícil distinguir
donde empieza el cielo
y termina el mar.

And it's difficult to tell
where the sea ends
and the sky begins.

*The music continues. They hum and drink Coca-Cola. A pigeon flies in and lands near them as the lights slowly fade to black.*